The *EcoHerbalist's Fieldbook*

Wildcrafting in the Mountain West

by Gregory L. Tilford

Mountain Weed Publishing
Conner, Montana

Copyright©1993 Gregory L. Tilford
All Rights Reserved

Edited by Mary Wulff-Tilford
Botanical Illustrations in Text by Richard W. Tyler
All photos and book design are by the author.

Mountain Weed Publishing Co.
HC 33, Box 17
Conner, MT 59827

10 9 8 7 6 5 4 3 2

Printed in the United States of America
by Bookcrafters of Chelsea, Michigan

Library of Congress Card Catalog Number: 93-80091

ISBN: 0-9638638-7-8

This book was composed and typeset using solar energy.

Cover Illustration: *Angelica species* by Richard W. Tyler

A Few Words About This Book...

It has taken me 25 years as an herbalist to wash away the previous three decades I lived in Los Angeles. The first decade was spent wallowing in the Great Outdoors, running stores and gathering wild herbs to sell in them (...what a life!). The next decade was spent learning about human beings, physiology, pharmacology, and grand intellectual concepts that I could take semi-seriously, and tell to students and patients that took them a bit more seriously (...what a life!).

The last few years, however, I started to notice the cattle, the mining, the clear cutting... and then I noticed the footprints of the campers and backpackers. Then I started to notice that some of the places I had taken students to in previous years were depleted of the very plants I showed them. Then I started to notice the current footprints of the two dozen people I was showing herbs to. Now I find I am starting to notice MY footprints. I no longer go further into the mountains to find new stands of what used to be abundant lower down the canyons. Instead I have tried to learn to use those herbs that are abundant, homely, and like people.

The EcoHerbalist's Fieldbook by Gregory Tilford defines and answers these very questions that took me all these years to even know how to ask. He ponders the questions of what can be spared, how to harvest and allow the ecology to recover in its own way, and how to view our actions as part of a network of subsequent reactions. Walk softly and carry no stick.

The fifty herbs in this caring book will supply all the main functions you need from plant medicines. Where they grow, how common they are, how they can and cannot be gathered, how best to prepare and use them, and your own responsibility towards them (and yourself) is carefully dealt with. Following the guidelines in the book would allow someone who used herbs frequently to gather what they wished in the same valley, year after year, without altering the ecology they were living within.

Michael Moore, Albuquerque, N.M.

This book is dedicated to the true Elders and teachers of the Earth, who through their innocence, perseverance, and unconditional love and sacrifice we can all find hope and well-being into the future...

DISCLAIMER

Dear Reader: The information in this book is intended to inspire, not prescribe. It is the author's, editor's and publisher's wishes that this book will help you along your personal paths to wellness, but no liability can be assumed by any of these parties for any therapies initiated by the reader or his/her assignees.

Acknowledgements

I believe that no one person on Earth is capable of completing a book without the influence of several allies. In fact, this book represents my ability to convey not only my own opinions and insight, but those of countless individuals (human and otherwise) that have inspired me to begin writing in the first place. Without these allies, this book would not exist. Of these allies, certain names and faces stand out and will never be forgotten... and I profoundly thank these people on behalf of myself and the plants and animals that will benefit from this book:

My wife, Mary, for her physical, spiritual, and inspirational support throughout this project. It was she who inspired me to look deeper into a reconnection with Earth through herbalism.

My Mother, Naomi... who's creativity, imagination, and loving patience taught me how to truly appreciate the wonders of Nature. Without her support this book would not have happened.

James Green... although our aquaintance is personally brief, your love and respect of our plant allies has inspired me and strengthened my spirit.

Janice Schofield... for advice and guidance that greatly benefited the design of this book.

Richard Tyler... for his talent and generosity.

Charles and Jessica... two caring people who helped to inspire me by opening their doors to me and my teaching.

Michael Moore... for his eternal contributions to

i

herbalists and herbalism.

Susun Weed... for her support, insight, and the spiritual alliances she has helped me to realize with our plant companions.

Rosemary Gladstar... for her infinite gifts of kindness and caring for humanity and Mother Earth.

To the learners that have attended Mary's and my classes... your attention and eagerness to learn about Nature's offerings has encouraged me to continue along my own path of learning.

And most of all I thank the plants, animals, insects, and the forces of Nature that have instilled within my heart a depth of love and wonder that extends beyond my imagination.

Table of Contents

Acknowledgements i

INTRODUCTION I

1: About this Book and its Format 1

THE REGION COVERED BY THIS BOOK 2
EXPLANATION OF FORMAT 3

2: EcoHerbalism: A Symbiotic Relationship of Earth & Herbalist 13

RECOGNIZING THE DISCONNECTED CHILD 13
TAMING THE ANTHROPOCENTRIC BEAST 16

3: Of Ethics and Impact 19

THE VALUE OF ETHICAL GUIDELINES 19
THE LIMITATIONS OF ETHICAL GUIDELINES
        WITHIN THE NATURAL REALM 20
WEBSTER AND ROGET WERE NOT ECOHERBALISTS 21
MULTI-LEVEL HUMAN IMPACT 21
THE REALITIES OF RESEEDING WHAT WE HARVEST 27
THE CONCEPT OF BIOREGIONAL HERBALISM 27
MAINTAINING RECORDS 28

Contents

4: *Medicinal Plant Companions of the Mountain West* 31

Alumroot 33
Angelica 39
Arnica 46
Balsamroot 51
Bee Balm 56
Burdock 60
Catnip 65
Cat's Paw 69
Chickweed 73
Cleavers 78
Clematis 84
Coptis 88
Cow Parsnip 94
Dandelion 99
Echinacea 104
Elderberry 107
False Solomon's Seal 112
Fireweed 116
Goldenrod 121
Horehound 126
Horsetail 130
Hound's Tongue 136
Juniper 141
Lomatium 146
Motherwort 153

Mullein 158
Oregon Grape 163
Osha´ 168
Penstemon 173
Pineapple-weed 177
Pipsissewa 182
Plantain 188
Poplar 193
Pyrola 199
Raspberry 205
Rattlesnake Plantain 210
Red Root 212
Sage 216
Self Heal 220
Shepherd's Purse 224
Stinging Nettle 230
St. John's Wort 237
Uva-ursi 242
Valerian 248
Wild Ginger 253
Wild Rose 258
Wild Strawberry 262
Willow 266
Yarrow 271
Yellow Dock 275

Appendices

I: BIBLIOGRAPHY & RECOMMENDED READING 281
II: THE ECOHERBALIST'S SOURCE LIST 284
III: GLOSSARY 289
IV: GENERAL INDEX 292
    About the Author, Editor & Artist

INTRODUCTION

The intended purpose of this book is to help fill two voids. One void exists on the bookshelf and in the backpack: the ever-present absence of accessible information that prompts us to carry more bookweight than bodyweight into wildcrafting expeditions. Although this book probably *will not* reduce your packweight (we all know that wildcrafting without at least three books in tow is pure folly), it *will* supplement your field library with comprehensive information that is specific to the concerns of wildcrafting medicinal plants.

I have found that most herbals contain little or no information regarding the actual gathering of plants, and very few address the issue of ethics. Although there are a few books written specifically as wildcrafting guides, they tend to be limited to plant identification and a narrowly viewed set of ethical guidelines.

This book is based upon a deep-ecology philosophy perspective that places us as *students*, not *dictators* of Earth's biocommunity. It is designed to stimulate the herbalist's ability to look much deeper into the ecosystems he or she interacts with during wildcrafting ventures. This book also serves as a field notebook that the herbalist can use to monitor and record impact, regrowth, and biological interdependencies within his or her bioregion.

The second void I hope to fill with this book (at least in part) lies within each and every one of us... the inherent

I

Introduction

chasm of disconnection between humanity and Nature.

As more people turn to Nature for sources of peace and healing, the commercialized mayhem of our planet continues. And despite the good intentions and efforts of those who love and care about the Earth and her children, a cumulative snowball of impact upon the planet continues to grow in the wake of a rapidly growing human population.

By and large, our efforts to manage Earth (and even ourselves) have failed. Humanity's sciences have enabled us to rationalize and challenge our intellect, but they provide no true substitutes for natural process. In *reality*, many of our scientific efforts to correct what we have damaged in the environment have resulted in nothing more than deeper levels of disaster. Perhaps it is time to stop dishing out orders and to listen to what the Earth and our planetary companions have to say. It's time to *reconnect*; time to *begin* our learning from the true elders of the Earth.

As herbalists we have already made a tentative reconnection with the Earth through the generosities of our plant allies. As *self-reliant* herbalists we have strengthened our reconnection by assuming more responsibility for our consumption and our impact. As we learn more about the plants we gather and the true wonders of *their* world, our level of appreciation and understanding intensifies... and so does our connection with nature. It is this level of learning, understanding, and subsequent reconnection that this book focuses upon.

I believe that all of today's environmental problems are borne from two aspects of humanity... our snowballing furor into over-population, and our collective desire to control the universe *(anthropocentricity)*. The human population issue is one that invariably leads me into a lengthy circle of verbose frustration... so I'll leave *that* book to another, braver soul.

Anthropocentricity has taken us on a journey away from the natural world on a skyrocket fueled by ignorance denial, and greed. As a self-reliant herbalist you have

II

Introduction

already turned the rocket around. Your journey toward a reunion with nature began when you recognized, accepted, and employed the healing powers of plants. Now I challenge you to take your journey a step farther; to assume a more *inclusive* role in the natural realm that has already fed your well-being.

Unlike others, this book is not intended to help you feel absolved from the impacts of your wildcrafting. It is intended to help you realize your new relationship with Nature; to cultivate a deeper level of personal and natural awareness.

It is for those of us that are ready to take the next step *backward* toward a greener life... and a greener planet.

For Mollie, my beloved friend and my teacher of all that really matters in this world. Green blessings to you wherever you are...

Part 1
About this Book and its Format

In order to use this book in the manner it is intended, it is imperative that you read the following chapters, *EcoHerbalism: A Symbiotic Relationship of Earth & Herbalist,* and *Of Ethics and Impact* in their entirety. It is these pages that contain the essence of what this book is about. This book is *not* intended to provide herbalists with all of the answers to the questions of ethical wildcrafting. To provide such answers, one would have to equate universal solutions from an infinite set of variables. Nothing in Nature is absolute... *and there is no such thing as a universal answer.* This is a workbook... a starting point from which you can: 1) begin to expand your knowledge of wild medicinal plants, and 2) develop and intensify your awareness as both a plant consumer *and* a member of the bio-community. This book is incomplete... in fact it represents only an outline and a reference base. It is up to you, the Ecoherbalist, to complete your own, personal edition...based on *your* insight and experience.

The technical information regarding botany and the

THE ECOHERBALIST'S FIELDBOOK

making and use of herbal medicines is based upon empirical information and the opinions, observations, and experiences of the author, his wife Mary *(whom is foremost the herbalist in my life)*; and the research of a long, *long* list of knowledgeable and effective herbalists. It is *not* necessarily based upon modern scientific validation, and is *certainly not* based upon western/allopathic principles of medicine.

Throughout this book I have left blank space everywhere possible for the scribbling of your valuable ideas and observations. Several record formats are included for your personal convenience and to supplement the effectiveness of this book's written text. I have written this book as simply as possible in recognition of other *field guides* that require a supplemental twenty pound Dictionary of Scientific Terminology (or a botany professor) to decipher their content. Unfortunately, some of the descriptive aspects of herbs and wildcrafting require specialized vocabulary, so I have included a glossary.

THE REGION COVERED BY THIS BOOK

At least a third of all herbs outlined within this book can be found to some extent throughout the contiguous United States, Western Canada, and Alaska. 50% to 75% of them can be found in the mountain areas of California, Nevada, Arizona, and New Mexico. Over 75% of the herbs in this book can be found in Alaska, the Rocky Mountains from Colorado through Wyoming, and east from the western edge of the Oregon and Washington Cascades to the west slope of the Rockies in Idaho.

All of the plants in this book can be found in Western Montana.

The species and abundance of each outlined herb varies greatly between micro-ecosystems and micro-climates. Plant densities also vary according to factors such as commercial impact and urban development.

2

EXPLANATION OF FORMAT (Part 4)

In Part 4 of this book I have included a total of 17 reference headings and subheadings for each outlined herb.

Common Name

The common name of an herb appears in large, bold letters at the top-center of the first page of each herb outline.

Botanical (Latin) Name & Family

Centered directly below the common name in **Bold Italics** is the latin name (genus and species), and the Family name, which may or may not coincide with your other botanical references. There seems to be some sort of ego battle going on between botanists, as many families have two or more names. Compositae *or* Asteraceae for example; both represent the Sunflower Family.

Impact Level:

Here I have categorized the general impact vulnerability of each plant and plant habitat, based upon the nature of the plant and its environment, its roles within an ecosystem, and its current status in the wild relative to human pressure.

I have designed this sub-heading in shaded, large letters so it stands out and protects our plant friends. This is intended as a "quick reference" only. Some *Impact Level: 1* herbs may be scarce in some areas, in which case they would rate a higher number. My assignment of an impact level is based upon my research and observations of conditions within the collective bioregions of the North American Mountain West at the time I wrote this book.

Impact Level Ratings

Impact Level: 1:

This level applies to herbs that are abundant, have a forseeable future of healthy proliferation, and are generally resilient to human impact. Many herbs within this category

3

THE ECOHERBALIST'S FIELDBOOK

are aliens that are looked upon as troublesome weeds, and are usually not a critical source of animal forage or habitat.

Impact Level: 2
Common herbs that grow in abundance and are maintaining themselves well in the face of humanity, but play well-defined, critical roles in the maintenance of their respective ecosystems. Most wild plants fall within this category.

Impact Level: 3
Herbs that are particularly vulnerable to impact because of their growth and/or habitat characteristics, or due to environmental concerns such as habitat contamination or reduction.

Impact Level: 4
Herbs which are already threatened or endangered and should not be gathered. I have included herbs under this category for the sole purpose of protecting them.

OTHER NAMES
Included under this sub-heading are other common names for each herb.

DESCRIPTION
This part provides a basic description of the herb in simple terms. It is not intended to serve as the only reference you should use when identifying an herb, but as a supplement to at least two or three others.
Information printed **in boldface represents the plant characteristics that I find particularly useful in their identification; or information that distinguishes the plant from a poisonous look-alike.**
The descriptive plant information in this book pertains to the species and identifying characteristics that I am familiar

4

About this Book

with, and specifically those which I believe are common to the primary region covered by this book.

HABITAT
This section describes the generalities of each plant's common habitat. The chosen habitat of a species may vary bioregionally and between micro-climates, depending upon the adaptability of the plant. For example, in the Southern Rockies the herb *Osha* is found almost exclusively at elevations above 8000', whereas it can be found as low as 5000' in the Northern Rockies. Plants that require shade and constant moisture (such as Cow Parsnip) and are common to wet, dark forested areas in the San Jacinto Mountains of Southern California may also be found in sunny, open meadows in areas with high annual precipitation and colder climates, such as in the coastal forests of British Columbia and Alaska.

The variances between micro-climates within a single bioregion can be extreme, particularly at northern latitudes. Where Mary and I live in Western Montana, temperatures and precipitation may commonly vary as much as 30% within thirty miles of our cabin. Depending upon a plant's adaptability, these climatic variances sometimes result in plant communities that have adjusted themselves to survive in a habitat that differs from the collective norm of the species. The result: a specially adapted sub-species.

ACTIONS
The term "actions" relates to the specific medicinal functions of an herb (ie., analgesic: helps to reduce pain). This book is not intended to serve as a primary reference of herbal applications, but as field workbook and reference that is specific to the concerns of wildcrafting. This section serves as "quick-glance" cross reference that you can use to determine which plants within your bioregion may be adaptable to your needs.

While this book briefly lists some of the most commonly employed actions of each plant, it generallly does

THE ECOHERBALIST'S FIELDBOOK

not outline all of the specifics of each action. Nor does it provide an in-depth assessment of each plant's specific affinities to particular systems of the human body. A working knowledge of plant actions and their medicinal affinities are essential to effective herbal therapy. The books that I have recommended under *"Technical References"* at the end of each herb outline serve as good starting points from which to customize your personal therapeutic approaches.

If you are not yet aquainted with the terms that are relative to herbal actions, I strongly recommend that you study them in the **Glossary**. An understanding of these actions and your recognition of the terminology will greatly simplify and enrich your therapeutic efforts.

PROPAGATION & GROWTH CHARACTERISTICS

This section represents my research and experiences relating to the cultivation and natural reproduction characteristics of each plant. It is intended to assist you in your endeavors to reseed the plants you harvest, in a manner that parallels the natural process as closely as I find possible. This section also serves to stimulate a deep awareness of the often delicate natural balances that are required to assure a plant's survival. I go into the subject of reseeding much deeper in **Part 3: Of Ethics and Impact**, under the subtitle: **The Realities of Reseeding What We Harvest**.

I encourage the development of an extensive herb garden, whenever and wherever possible. This section addresses many of the specifics you need in adapting your favorite herbs to the home garden.

GATHERING SEASON AND GENERAL GUIDELINES

This section outlines ethical and ecologically insightful methods for the gathering of each herb. The season recommended for the gathering of each herb is chosen first in consideration of the plant's particular needs, and secondly in consideration of medicinal potency.

If you have already read the following chapters, you

6

About this Book

know by now that I truely dislike the term *guideline*. This section is not intended to impose "a concrete set of rules" concerning the ethical harvest of wild herbs, but to instill a deeper perception of our impacts. The practices that I am conveying to you are those which Mary and I have employed with very favorable results, *after* experiencing the often frustrating and damaging consequences of our trials and errors. It is my hope that in passing on these "guidelines" you will be able to circumvent some of the trial-and-error that is at the expense of our plant and animal allies. It is important to remember that despite our past successes, the impact reduction methods I have outlined here *are not* necessarily foolproof, nor do they represent all possible solutions to this very complex issue. Use your imagination and natural insight, and figure out more ways to reduce impact... then spread your knowledge. I'd love to hear from you.

CARE AFTER GATHERING
        This section outlines preparation and storage methods that will assure optimum potency, shelf life, and usefulness of the herbs you gather. All of these considerations equate back to the well-being of our plant allies, as they reduce waste. Tinctures, oils, infusions, and other herbal formulas that I have outlined here are generally universal throughout the western herbal community, and are based upon empirical and scientific data.
        I strongly encourage you to consult other references in addition to this one, and to identify any other formulas that may be pertinent to your specific needs.

COMMON COMPANION HERBS
        This section provides you with a list of other medicinal plants that may be sharing space with the particular herb you are after. It is only a small list of possibilities, and like Nature itself, contains no absolutes.

THE ECOHERBALIST'S FIELDBOOK

PLANT/ANIMAL INTERDEPENDENCE

The essence of EcoHerbalism is a deeper awareness of how every living thing relates to all others. All organisms, from amoeba to moose, are in some capacity dependent upon one another within an ecosystem. This section is intended to deepen your awareness of how each plant contributes to the livelihood of its particular biocommunity. It is *not* an entire account, but a basis from which you can expand your personal insight. The information contained in this section is based upon my observations and those of other herbalists and naturalists.

This section will help you look beyond the narrow focus of common resource management practices (which I talk about in more length later) and into some of the delicate balances in which each plant is involved.

The survival of the collective being we call an *ecosystem* is dependent upon Nature's delicate balance of biodiversity. Each plant, animal, insect, and microorganism can be viewed as a small but critical piece of a very complex puzzle... if one piece is taken away, the entire puzzle may fall apart. Through my conveyed observations and experience, I hope to encourage you to embark upon an unending journey into new levels of natural awareness.

IMPACT CONSIDERATIONS

In this section I have written about wildcrafting impact considerations that I feel are specifically at issue with each particular herb. Again, this section represents only a limited list of impact and solution possibilities. It provides a basis for further investigation into the specifics of your bioregion.

PHOTO REFERENCES

Here I have listed some good references that you can use to positively identify the herb in the field. I have included this section so that you can access the information you need without first searching through twenty books (I have done it for you!).

8

About this Book

TECHNICAL REFERENCES

Under this sub-heading I have listed some good references that are specific to the employment of the herb. This list provides quick access to pertinent *materia medica* and other useful information about the herb, and eliminates lengthy research.

STAND LOCATIONS AND FIELD NOTES

At the end of each herb outline you will find a blank record format and room for your personal field notes. This *stand location* format allows you to keep accurate records of each specific herb stand you have come across within your bioregion *(fig. 1.1)*. It is designed to act as a convenient index to your personal records.

I have also provided examples of a *wildcrafting site record* (*fig. 1.2)* and a corresponding *wildcrafting log (fig. 1.3)* on pages 11 & 12 to illustrate one possibility for a record-keeping system.

Similar records can be kept on 5"x7" index cards, or in a spiral notebook... they don't need to be fancy, just *detailed and accurate.*

If you like the format presented in figs. 1.2 & 1.3, *you are welcome to copy them word-for word, or you can order the reproducible, blank forms, for $2.50, from:*

Mountain Weed Publishing/Forms
HC 33, Box 17
Conner, MT. 59827

THE ECOHERBALIST'S FIELDBOOK

STAND LOCATIONS

Date of Discovery	Location and Description of Stand	Site Record #
6-15-91	HILLTOP SOUTH OF OSIER SPRINGS, ½ MILE NORTH OF FOREST RD #223	12

fig. 1.1 *This format is handy for recording the precise location for quick and easy future reference.*

WILDCRAFTING SITE RECORD
Site# 12

Location of Site: HILLTOP S. OF OSIER SPRINGS, 1/2 MI. N.
OF FOREST RD 223 TURNOFF *Date of Initial Visit:* 6-15-91
Herbs of Interest: BALSAMROOT AND YARROW

Size and Condition of Plant Stands: LARGE STANDS OF OLDER PLANTS,
IN GOOD CONDITION WITH ALOT OF YOUNGER GROWTH DOWNSLOPE

Weather and Growth Conditions During and Preceeding Initial Visit: UNSEASONABLY
WARM FOR JUNE ; APRIL & MAY ABOVE AVG. PRECIP.
Natural Characteristics of Site (degree of slope. elevation, exposure, water sources, type of forest, companion plants. etc.): STEEP, DRY, OPEN GRASSLAND WITH A
FEW PONDEROSA PINES ; SOUTHERN EXPOSURE ; NO GROUND
WATER VISIBLE ; LOTS OF KNAPWEED AND DOGBANE.
Access to Stand: 1/2 MILE WALK ON GOOD FOOTTRAIL
Proximity to roadways, Powerlines, Etc.: 1/2 MI (DIRT ROAD) *Hx of herbicides/pesticides:* NONE
Evident Human Impact: HILLTOP WAS SELECTIVELY LOGGED ABOUT
5 YRS. AGO (1986) ; OLD COW PIES ARE PRESENT
Possible Future Human Impact: PERHAPS MORE CATTLE GRAZING

Natural Impacts Observed or Anticipated (insect infestation. heavy forage due to hard winter. drought. migratory abnormalities. etc.): GRASSHOPPERS ARE HATCHING
EARLY AND ABUNDANTLY — MAY CAUSE SOME DEFOLIATION
OF BALSAMROOT LEAVES/FLOWERS.
Animals/insects that are Present or Evident at Site (note tracks. scat. nests. bed areas. etc.): DEER & ELK DROPPINGS EVERYWHERE. REDTAILED HAWK
NEST IN TREE, SOUTH OF HILLTOP.

Noticeable Plant/Animal Interdependencies (nibbled leaves. habitat. nesting material plant. cover. etc.): SOME BALSAMROOT LEAVES ARE NIBBLED ; BALSAMROOT
GROWTH PROBABLY PROVIDES PREY COVER (HAWK IS WATCHING!)

Species and Quantities Gathered During Initial Visit: NONE — WILL MONITOR
UNTIL LATE-SUMMER GATHERING TIME.

OTHER NOTES:
ROCKSLIDE ON NORTH EXPOSURE IS UNSTABLE AND SHOULD
BE AVOIDED.

fig. 1.2 The "Wildcrafting Site Record" format enables the EcoHerbalist to establish a comprehensive record base from which ecological changes can be observed and recorded.

WILDCRAFTING LOG
Site# 12

Date	Notes and Observations
7-31-91	MARY AND I HAD PICNIC ON HILLTOP, LEAVES ON BALSAMROOT ARE DYING BACK. YARROW IS READY TO PICK. NO NEW IMPACT OBSERVED.
8-25-91	DUG ONE LARGE BALSAMROOT MIDWAY DOWN SOUTH HILL. PERIPHERAL PLANTS LEFT UNDISTURBED. ROOT IS STILL MOIST ; GOOEY INSIDE.
8-26-91	MADE 1 QUART TINCTURE FROM YESTERDAY'S ROOT.
6-15-92	VISITED SITE. A SMALL FIRERING HAS APPEARED ON TOP OF THE HILL — PROBABLY LAST FALL'S HUNTING CAMP. BALSAMROOT ; YARROW IS JUST COMING UP. LOTS OF EVIDENCE OF DEER FEEDING ; BEDDING DOWN — SPRING GRASSES LOOK ABUNDANT.
7-22-92	BALSAMROOT IN GENERALLY GOOD HEALTH, BUT FORAGE GRASSES ARE SCARCER THAN ANTICIPATED. FOUND BEAR SCAT ; EVID. OF ROOT FORAGE AT BOTTOM OF SOUTH HILL. PLANTS ON TOP HAVE BEEN HEAVILY ATTACKED BY INSECTS. HAWK NEST (SITE REC IS GONE. YARROW IS ABUNDANT, READY, ; I GATHERED 4 OZ. OF FRESH FLOWERS. NO NEW HUMAN IMPACT. NO COWS.
6/17/93	WET SPRING HAS BROUGHT A PROLIFERATION OF NEW GROWTH TO SITE — PARTICULARLY YARROW AND FORAGE GRASSES. BALSAMROOT IS UP ; LOOKING GOOD. MR. HAWK HAS RETURNED TO NORTH SIDE OF HILLTOP. HUNTING CAMP UNCHANGED ; APPEARS UNUSED LAST FAL
8/20/93	DUG ONE LARGE BALSAMROOT FROM BOTTOM/CENTER OF HILLSIDE. HARVEST FROM 8-25-91 SHOWS NO SIGN OF VICARIOUS IMPACT, ETC.

Fig. 1.3 The Wildcrafting Log updates and supplements your original, detailed site record and is updated during every subsequent visit to the wildcrafting site.

Part 2
EcoHerbalism:
A Symbiotic Relationship
of Earth & Herbalist

RECOGNIZING THE DISCONNECTED
CHILD

To most people, *getting back to nature* means going camping or living in the woods. Many of us feel reconnected to the natural world when we engage in our favorite outdoor activities, such as fishing or backpacking. A few of us take our desire to reconnect a step farther and choose to live remotely in the mountains or deserts with few modern luxuries. In the sense that we are expressing a respect, concern, or appreciation toward the natural world, such activities and lifestyles *do* connect us with nature... at least in our hearts and minds. But how do we truly relate to the natural world as members of the Earth community? Do we really *reconnect* with nature when we rejoice in the lingering sweet fragrances of a cedar forest, or do we merely fantasize a reunion?

THE ECOHERBALIST'S FIELDBOOK

Before we can begin to answer these questions we must first identify what we *are* in relation to everything around us. We must search ourselves from within and take a long, hard look at what we, as humans, have become. Then comes the painful part... *we must accept what we find.* I believe that then, and only then, we can choose a direction towards closer co-existence with the natural world.

It is very likely that the first (and perhaps the last) human to have served an inclusive, natural role on this planet was covered with hair and dragged his knuckles. Since then we have progressively evolved (both physically and psychologically) away from the natural world. We are a creature that has strived to defy and conquer the powers of nature since the beginning of our history. With fire we learned to warm ourselves against winter in absence of adequate shelter. We invented the wheel to exploit the forces of gravity, enabling ourselves to avoid strenuous exercise. The list of our comfort accomplishments goes on and on, and through our intellectual development and constant yearning to control the universe, it appears that we have genetically altered ourselves into a creature that can no longer adapt naturally to any environment on Earth.

Generation upon generation of intellectual development and subsequent technology has instilled within us an inherent sense of independence from Nature, and as a result we are now naturally inept creatures. In order to fulfill our physical and psychological needs, we must supplement our bodies and lifestyles with artificial enhancements. For instance, when we venture from the synthetic environments we call our homes, we must protect our vulnerable bodies from exposure to the elements with the artificial outer skins we call *clothing*. If we drink water that contains certain microorganisms (ones that have been naturally present for millions of years) we become sick, as our bodies are accustomed to water which has been altered by our own device. Psychologically we have become creatures of directed thought, greed, and self-indulgent needs

A Symbiotic Relationship

that have absolutely nothing to do with a natural process, and sensually we have tuned out most of our consciousness and all but the most rudimentary of instincts. Thousands of years of intellectually-biased perception and natural indifference has instilled within us a lofty attitude of being invincible, leaving our senses dulled and out-of-focus. Most of us live within the confines of our racing, analytical minds; a state of "tunnel vision" that tunes out our peripheral vision and our conscious ability to detect subtle noises and odors... most of the time our brains are focused entirely upon the *thought of the moment.* For instance, when we walk on a rocky trail we tend to focus almost entirely upon what is directly in front of us, in close proximity. In so doing, we miss the subtle snap of a twig and the brief flash of brown that represents a deer bounding into cover from our left or right. This sensual state of paralysis accurately illustrates a disconnection with the natural universe, as does our physical ineptness. A wild animal in such a condition could not survive.

By recognizing that our disconnection with Nature goes far beyond just our attitudes, we can assume a much deeper level of responsibility for our actions. My wife and I have strived to live as close to nature as possible. We have left financial security and the comforts of modern living behind to pursue our love for the Earth and all of her complexities. We live, eat, and sleep with the forest around us, and in doing this we have sadly learned to accept that as humans, we will always be alien to the plants and animals we love. But at the same time we have also learned how to be much *kinder* and *respectful* aliens. As we learn the truths of what we are and set aside our denial driven fantasies we recognize that we are not viewed by wildlife as mere predators, but as strange unpredictable *things* from another universe. I have observed relationships between prey and predator, and I have found that it is one of inherent awareness, understanding and respect. But the relationship between humanity and wild animals is very different... it is one of confusion, anxiety, and fear. Grizzly bears and other predators are commonly seen browsing in

THE ECOHERBALIST'S FIELDBOOK

peace, side-by-side with the very animals they prey upon. Their active, natural role during such instances is obviously well-defined. But *our mere presence*, regardless of our attitude or intent, proves disruptive when introduced into a natural scenario. Every time we venture into wilderness we interrupt natural processes, such as feeding patterns or an animal's mating ritual, because we are so different. Most of what we do is in bold contrast to the natural scheme... we build our dwellings from naturally alien materials atop natural habitats, and clear the land to introduce alien plants. We travel around in loud, metal things that breathe fire, walk on our hind legs, and undoubtedly smell weird (if not foul).

As herbalists, we have demonstrated to ourselves a willingness to humbly accept a natural offering of well-being that has existed for all living things since the beginning of life on Earth, and thus we have taken a large step toward reconnecting on a very integral level. It is well known that most of our companion organisms are also herbalists, and we have chosen to share a common bond with them. We have become involved with their community, but we must recognize that it is *their community*, and that *they are the true stewards.*

Our plant and animal companions know that we are different, and by nature very dangerous. The learning is up to us. We must accept the facts of our species and put denial-driven fantasies aside if we wish to deepen our natural reunion with the Earth. We must learn to give as we receive, as all other life on Earth does, in a manner that serves the entire bio-community and not just our own.

What the elders of the natural world do as their blood flows, we the children must figure out.

TAMING THE ANTHROPOCENTRIC BEAST

As members of humanity, we have all inherited a mind that to a varying degree puts human purpose at the center of what we consider the universe. Although we emotionally deny it, we are all guilty of being anthropocentric. It is part of our

16

A Symbiotic Relationship

nature.

To illustrate this issue, let's do a short exercise: Consider the philosophy behind our National Parks... they are *designed* to preserve a *natural resource* in a pristine condition *for our enjoyment.* The primary consideration here is that of human recreation, *not* the preservation of wild lands in respect to the plants and animals dependent upon them.

Webster's Dictionary defines the term *natural resource* as: "A necessary or beneficial material source, as of timber or a mineral deposit, occurring in nature".

Right now, you may be experiencing another inherency... an emotional defense mechanism that is perhaps telling you to think, *"I don't like that definition... I believe that National Parks should be for the protection of plants and animals... not just human recreational interests,"* or perhaps you have concluded, *"I think that National Parks provide people with opportunities to appreciate and respect the wonders and grandeur of Nature... both worlds benefit."*

Regardless of your opinion, by now you have *rationalized* the issue to your satisfaction. In reaching your own opinion, your final aim was to satisfy how you feel. Although this was not a physical exercise, the process it illustrates dictates our lives. Our morals, religion, family values, recycling efforts, or whatever are conceived from an inherent rationalization process that is designed to make *ourselves feel comfortable.* Forestry presents another excellent example. We cut down trees, then plant a tree farm. Happy with the thick row of trees we have propagated, we learn to deny the fact that the forest is actually gone forever... no matter how many trees we plant. We have satisfied our guilt, not the *real* need for a natural forest. What we drink, eat, say, do, and believe is based upon analytical, emotionally-driven self-justifications.

Unlike our plant and animal companions, we live to satisfy our reasoning, which in turn is largely dictated by emotion. Animals and plants contribute to natural balances without this burden of analytical thinking. A mountain lion does not have to emotionally justify its diet... it eats its prey

THE ECOHERBALIST'S FIELDBOOK

out of instinctive, natural purpose. It does not have to figure out where it needs to cull an over-population of deer, nor does it need to figure out how many to take... it just *does* out of Nature's intent and design. I am not suggesting that animals are unfeeling, thoughtless creatures... they are quite the contrary. They simply have not been consumed by the so-called "gift" of intellectual development.

As humans we are bound within the confines of a mind that has developed inward; into a quagmire of logic and emotion that has focused our attention away from natural realities. We are egotistical, emotional creatures who have lost most of the instinct required to be natural role players. The anthropocentric beast within each of us inhibits our primordial instincts and clouds our ability to understand how the natural world operates, and in doing so it prohibits us from assuming truely inclusive natural roles. But by taming the beast, we *can* begin a mutually beneficial and loving relationship with Nature. *First* we must understand and accept what we have become; then we can open new doors into natural awareness. We *must* confront the anthropocentric beast that lives just below the surface of our consciousness, then realize and accept it's existence, because when the beast is brought into conscious light it becomes much tamer. And by trying to understand it, we can look beyond the human bubble and see the true, unfiltered realities of our planet and how it operates.

We cannot expect to kill the anthropocentric beast, but we can certainly keep it on a leash while we learn to harmonize with our plant and animal companions. And although we may never step out of our clothes and houses to re-enter the natural universe, our clearer, deeper understanding and respect for nature and our many elders will contribute to many mutual benefits between humanity and the natural world. A symbiosis will be born.

I challenge you to leash your beast within, and to listen, see, smell, hear, and feel what Nature has to teach you... through the magic of medicinal plants.

18

Part 3
Of Ethics and Impact...

Impact: *The strong effect exerted by one person or thing on another.*

...Roget's

THE VALUE OF ETHICAL GUIDELINES
Ethical guidelines are essential in maintaining a basis of moral and practical conduct. They put fundamental aspects of impact reduction into a cognizant format that is easy to follow. The essence of ethical wildcrafting is the ability to gather wild plants in a manner that is conducive to the plants' well-being. Ethical guidelines provide a basis from which we can work toward achieving this goal, within a limited perspective.

For your reference, I have included a list of ethical guidelines at the end of this chapter.

THE LIMITATIONS OF ETHICAL GUIDELINES WITHIN THE NATURAL REALM

If employed as the only means of reducing impact, ethical guidelines are only effective within the limits of self-government and a narrow scope of basic human insight.

In my experience, I have found that most wildcrafters use simple, mathematical formulas and preconceived ethical guidelines to keep their impact at a minimum. *"Take 3 of every 10 plants, scatter the seeds, and leave the rest"* is one formula I hear often.

Sounds simple enough, but is the aforementioned formula effective in impact reduction, or does it merely serve as a means to pacify our conscience? Have we addressed the issue of impact completely, as members of the bio-community, or are we simply imposing superficial, ethical standards in order to satisfy our emotional needs? I propose that we leash the anthropocentric beast for awhile and explore some of the *realities* of this very complex issue...

The degree and nature of human impact upon an ecosystem varies according to an endless combination of conditions and circumstances. The number of leaves, roots, flowers, etc. that we take in relation to a stand of plants represents only a few of many things to consider before setting off on a wildcrafting expedition. A simple mathematical formula, and adherence to a set of rules (as good as they may be) amounts to nothing more than "ego-aspirin" for our guilty conscience, unless we factor in the countless variables. Many of these variables include the human factor. An example would be gathering from a stand of plants that has already been impacted by another wildcrafter. In addition to human influences, we must also consider natural variables, like grasshopper infestations, forest fires, or animal forage, before we can effectively take responsibility for our actions. Again, we must remember the Disconnected Child; what may come naturally to a bird or deer may require us to study, analyze, and experiment... and with experimentation comes the high

Of Ethics and Impact

costs of trial and error. Again we must bring the anthropocentric beast into light and realize that our purpose during such ventures is largely based upon *our* needs and not necessarily those of the ecosystem we are visiting. We must recognize that human reasoning is *not* a part of the natural process within the ecosystem, and we must accept an empathetic perspective that places our wildcrafting as an imposition to our plant and animal allies. Then, and only then can we begin to achieve the ability to view the true extent of our impact.

With our fantasies of natural inclusion set aside, we can more clearly confront, investigate, and in many instances *predict* our short and long-term impacts.

Because of our poorly adapted physical design, genetically altered instinctive capabilities, and intellectually corroded level of sensual awareness, the impact we often perceive as minor can have long-term, irreversible effects. A good example is erosion that results from our improper choice of footwear. We slip and slide while pursuing Alumroot on a steep hillside, and think nothing of the displaced stones and soil... until we discover that the same stand of plants has been washed away by spring run-off. Other impacts are harder to foresee, and some cannot be predicted at all.

Example: Gathering from a stand of plants that will soon be subjected to drought... or an exceptionally cold winter.

Where plants, animals and insects thoughtlessly migrate or adjust their growth and feeding patterns prior to such events, we remain oblivious to them. Although we cannot foresee such events, our awareness of their possibility brings about a stronger sense of responsibility and a more caring approach toward our herbal endeavors.

THE ECOHERBALIST'S FIELDBOOK

WEBSTER AND ROGET WERE NOT ECOHERBALISTS

Although I use the words "ethical" and "guidelines" throughout this book, I find both of these words ambiguous if used in a context of how Nature operates. Both words have a strong inference of some sort of human control. The word *ethical* means to conform to a set of principles perceived as right or wrong. In Nature these two human concepts do not exist... *there is no right or wrong,* there just *is.* The word *guideline* means to set a procedure or policy. In the natural world, the only policy is *to live,* and everything subsequent to living comes automatically through instinct and natural process. I use these words because they serve as a recognizable reference... *not* because I believe we can harmonize with Nature by imposing humanity's rules. Although strong ethical guidelines offer an essential starting point in the reduction of our impact, they do not address the entire scope of the issue.

The EcoHerbalist must try to understand natural processes and cooperate within the natural scheme of things. If we do not try to coexist within nature's way of doing things, we are accomplishing little more than romanticizing our exploitation.

MULTI-LEVEL HUMAN IMPACT

To help us visualize the realities of human impact I have broken it down into different levels of awareness and deliberation. It is my intent to stimulate within you a new insight that will bring you closer to our plant and animal companions through an enriched awareness and a deeper sense of responsibility. Human impact can be divided into three overlapping levels: *Intentional Impact, Unintentional Impact,* and *Vicarious Impact.*

1. Intentional Human Impact is impact that we intend to cause. The practice of wildcrafting herbs in itself represents an intentional impact upon particular plants. Although the severity of impact can be minimized by proper technique, a

22

Of Ethics and Impact

high level of awareness and a caring attitude, our harvest of plants *always* represents some degree of intentional impact.

Intentional impact is premeditated... a result of planned encroachment into an ecosystem. It is the level of impact that we have the most control over, as we can premeditate its reduction as well.

What we deem as intentional impact is relative to our individual levels of awareness, caring, and understanding. An intentional act requires conscious recognition *before* it is carried out, otherwise the act remains unintentional. For instance, if I choose to access a stand of plants with the use of a car, I take into consideration the nature and severity of the impact that will result. If I decide to use the car (which I would not!), then I am prepared to assume responsibility for my subsequent impact. The act is deliberate, so the impact can be reduced through careful planning. On the other hand, if I were to drive a car into the stand as an uncaring, oblivious slob, my impact would be largely unintentional and totally unrestrained. The difference between the two scenarios could be very significant, and although they are exaggerated (I hope!), they accurately illustrate the importance of achieving higher levels of natural awareness and understanding.

To put this into a more subtle perspective, we can look at the characteristics of our feet. When I venture onto a soft, moist meadow, I am consciously aware of the soil compaction that will result if I do not plan every step. But many people are unaware of how much damage human feet can do to the delicate plants and soil structures of such an environment, and they enter the meadow with no idea of the impact they are causing. In this instance the severity of their impact goes unchecked.

Since the intentional level of impact allows for proactive reduction efforts, it stands to reason that we need to keep our impact within this level whenever possible. *This is where everything I have rambled-on about in previous pages really begins to pay off...*because when we recognize and accept our natural shortcomings, we become more aware of our potential

THE ECOHERBALIST'S FIELDBOOK

to cause unintentional impact. This enables us to take a more proactive approach toward reducing our wildcrafting impact.

2. Unintentional Human Impact is impact that we are directly responsible for but fail to recognize while it is occurring. Everything I have already said about our inherent disconnection with Nature relates to this level of impact. We have already narrowed the gap between ourselves and the natural universe by confronting the condition of our species, such as the design of our feet and the importance of deliberate movement and soft footwear when moving about in a moist meadow. We may also realize that our presence alone is disruptive to wildlife... so now we move through the meadow more quietly. But how deep does our unintentional impact go? How much of the Nature/Humanity chasm can we transcend to put our impact into a conscious light?

The answer to these questions lies within each of us as individuals. Our access to these answers is regulated by how successful we are in developing our self-awareness and our desire to understand the ecosystems we are working within, *without* the interference of anthropocentric reasoning. We must strive to realize that plants, animals, insects, fish, weather, *everything* coexists in a tightly-knit, interdependent natural universe that is beyond anything that can be controlled by a set of our rules.

To provide you with some food for conscious thought, I have listed some unintentional impacts that are based upon our atrophied senses and out-of-tune mentalities:

*Loud Conversation...*is threatening or at least disruptive to wildlife. By interrupting animal and insect activities, natural balances can be disturbed. Wildcrafting in an area where the deer are fawning is one example; the plants you are removing may be interdependent with the deer you are disturbing, and the absence of the frightened families may create a serious imbalance within the micro-ecosystem.

24

Of Ethics and Impact

Antagonistic Activities... such as rock throwing or building a campfire is likely to have a strong, adverse psychological effect upon wildlife.

Poor Perception in peripheral vision... results in trampled plants and creatures that we could have stepped over... if only we had known they were there. Because we use only a fraction of our visual and perceptive capabilities, we fail to see much of the wildlife that is standing nearby.

Intellectually-focused Hearing that doesn't detect the sounds made by terrified animals that are scrambling away from us. Our hearing is generally tuned to sounds that we are familiar with or those that we consciously choose to hear.

Our Tuned-out Sense of Touch... We wear shoes to insure that we don't feel anything beneath our feet. Our footwear allows us to unknowingly trample dozens of plants and other organisms every day.

Our Noses... are generally mind-tuned to detect the familiar or the obvious. Although completely capable, the nose did not detect the nearby deer that has already evaded our eyes and ears.

The Screaming Pink and Yellow Shirt... that sends *all* living things screaming from the forest (including other wildcrafters). It is well known that many animals *do* see shades of color. Colors such as blue, red, and orange tend to contrast sharply against flora and fauna, adding to psychological impact.

3. Vicarious human impact... is unintentional impact that results when factors beyond our awareness compound an already existing impact, or an impact that has not yet occurred.

25

THE ECOHERBALIST'S FIELDBOOK

Examples:

✿ *Gathering plants prior to an unanticipated drought or other stressful conditions.*

✿ *Introduction of a plant where its proliferation competes with other species.*

✿ *Gathering in an area that is later heavily foraged due to poor forage availability in another area.*

✿ *Gathering from an area that later becomes subject to logging, grazing, or any other high-impact activity.*

✿ *Wildcrafting in an area that has already been impacted by other wildcrafters.*

In exploring this level of impact it is easy to see the futility in the *take three and leave seven* wildcrafting policy. Since we cannot look into a crystal ball and accurately predict the nature and extent of vicarious impact, it is potentially the most destructive and far-reaching. Therefore, we must *always* assume that whenever we create *any impact*, other effects of our actions will likely occur.

In view of the number of people that are taking to the woods for wholistic and exploitive purposes, we are faced with the scary reality of a vicarious impact "snowball effect". We cannot stop the "impact snowball" from gaining momentum unless we assume a proactive attitude as individuals. This means *trying our best to foresee future events and adjusting our acts accordingly.* Although this attitude cannot always prevent a snowball, our awareness of its potential and our willingness to take responsibility for it can reduce its initial size and velocity. Like all snowballs, the smaller we build them and the slower we roll them...the smaller the end result.

Of Ethics and Impact

THE REALITIES OF RESEEDING WHAT WE HARVEST

One of the ideas that many wildcrafters accept as an ethical guideline is the reseeding of areas from which we harvest to an extent of proliferation that exceeds its prior condition. By propagating more in a stand than existed before our visit, are we really reducing our impact, or merely creating a new one that appeals to our conscience? *Is the anthropocentric beast at work again?*

Please take a moment to think about this: Is the presence of fifty plants in a spot where only ten once grew necessarily beneficial to that patch of habitat? Or is it detrimental to natural balances and the requirements of companion organisms?

One of the major concepts I am trying to convey with this book is one which places our wildcrafting in a *cooperative* role, not one which "manages a resource". It is my belief that humanity's efforts to manage ecosystems has largely failed, and that our continuance of this governing attitude is resulting in a huge snowball of vicarious impact. Our perception of good deed may not always translate to the well-being of our plant and animal companions. Our kindhearted cultivation of plants in unnatural quantities could result in ecological damage that far exceeds the impact caused by the act of harvesting. In reality, the land may not be able to sustain increased growth. An area that becomes overpopulated with one plant may no longer be able to accommodate less competitive others.

Rather than think in numbers, we must learn to understand how prospective ecosystems maintain themselves, and try our best to work within Nature's methods. This means learning as much as we can about our respective bioregions on an intimate level.

Otherwise we have not yet escaped from our "tree farm mentalities"... and the anthropocentric beast still prevails.

THE CONCEPT OF BIOREGIONAL HERBALISM

If we are to participate in a truly symbiotic relationship with Nature, we must first open our hearts and minds to how

THE ECOHERBALIST'S FIELDBOOK

Nature works. This means we must spend time in the natural classroom that surrounds our home. We must re-educate our sensual abilities and sharpen our perceptive awareness in order to see, smell, hear, taste and feel how an ecosystem lives and dies. We must observe at an intimate level, and learn until our knowledge becomes instinct.

To study nature in such depth we must spend a long period of time within a segment of a specific bioregion. As our knowledge and understanding of this piece of Earth grows, so does our sense of being. It is from this posture of deep understanding and respect that we can be most effective in minimizing our impact. As we develop our relationship with a bioregion, we assume a greater sense of responsibility and concern for its well-being... we become attached. And although we remain separated by our intellectual and physical design, we can learn to live in a manner that benefits both worlds. After one has lived close to a specific natural community and has begun to understand how it operates, one realizes that the need to learn is unilaterally human. The willingness to coexist with humanity has always existed among our plant and animal companions. To reach a symbiotic relationship with them is not dependent upon what they can do for us, or us for them, but what we can do *together*.

MAINTAINING RECORDS

The maintenance of accurate, up-to-date field records is a crucial element of ethical conduct and in the reduction of impact *(pages 10-12)*. By keeping good records, we are able to accurately keep track of the long-term effects of our wildcrafting and monitor the constantly changing natural activities within specific micro-ecosystems. Without such records we are likely to forget our observations of many subtleties that can contribute to major changes within an ecosystem. For example, failure to remember the presence and foraging requirements of an herbivorous organism (anything from insect to moose) in an area we commonly harvest from may result in vicarious impact that could have

28

Of Ethics and Impact

been avoided. Records eliminate many of our unintentional impacts by putting them in conscious form.

The format I have composed on pages 10-12 enable the herbalist to establish and maintain accurate, updated, cross-referenced records of his or her activities and other developments as they occur in each stand of plants. If you choose to design your own record-keeping program, here are some suggested elements to consider...

Information Specific to Each Gathering Site:

* *The location of specific wildcrafting sites.*
* *The date of your first visit to each site and the date of each subsequent visit.*
* *The name (preferably the botanical name) of the specific plants you intend to harvest at each site.*
* *Comprehensive, detailed information that describes the natural characteristics of each site (riparian, dryland, alpine, subalpine, wooded, open hillside, etc.).*
* *Proximity of the site to roadways, powerlines.*
* *Any known history of pesticide/herbicide, and records of your verifications.*
* *The weather conditions during each visit (to help minimize vicarious impact).*
* *An inventory of insects and animals that you have observed during each visit to each site, and the noticeable effects of their presence.*
* *An inventory of companion plants you observe (the best you can do) during your first visit, and updates concerning their well-being at every subsequent visit.*

Information Specific to Your Actions:

* *The quantity of each specific herb harvested.*

* *The results of your last visit: visible, subsequent impact; regrowth and/or reseeding successes & failures.*
* *Your wildcrafting methods: how you gathered the herb(s) and cared for them afterward, with specific notes on how*

THE ECOHERBALIST'S FIELDBOOK

well the methods did or didn't work.

❊ *Up-to-date records pertaining to other impacts that have, will, or may occur anywhere near the harvest site, such as logging operations, new construction, RV use, aerial spraying, or impact from other wildcrafters.*

❊ *BOLD, QUICK-REFERENCES that bring to immediate attention any important impact/ethical considerations pertaining to the gathering site.*

❊ *Notes, notes, and more notes about anything that comes to mind during each visit...the more notes you take, the more quickly you will become familiar with your bioregion.*

Part 4
Medicinal Plant Companions
of
The Mountain West

Prayer of the Ancient Ones

Through the centuries I have stood
inhumed within the land that I feed and protect.
My breath is the basis of all life...
my branches a sanctuary for all who seek
shelter and the security of my supple strength.

I am a delegate of virtue...
the essence of well-being.
I give these gifts graciously
                        thoughtlessly

Let me not fall
to the selfish whims of fraudulent Gods.

...As Interpreted by a Student of the Earth

Alumroot

Heuchera species   Saxifrage Family

IMPACT LEVEL: 2

OTHER NAMES
Mountain Saxifrage, Alpine Heuchera, Poker Alumroot.

DESCRIPTION
A perennial with a short bloom duration, this plant is generally found as a cluster of leathery, ovate to heart-shaped basal leaves protruding from steep banks or rocky areas. Leaves are similar in appearance to currant leaves, and generally remain on the smaller side of their ½" to 3" range. Plants are usually small; 6" to 12" high when mature.

The flowers of Alumroot are small and cup-shaped, with five simple petals ranging in color from greenish-white to light pink. The leafless, erect flower stalks reach much higher than the leaf cluster; sometimes as high as 20", each bearing one to several flowers that often grow along just one side of the stalk. After a brief bloom period, the flower stalk often looks like a brown to rust-colored twig.

The root is proportionately large and covered with scaly, brown, dead plant material. The inner pith of the root is flesh-colored and has a very astringent/acidic flavor. The sour taste is due to its extremely high tannin content.

HABITAT
Alumroot is a high elevation, cliff-clinging little plant that is common on steep, rocky hillsides and forested areas that are generally shaded and moist most of the time. It needs rich organic matter at its roots for support in its often harsh environment, and is often found growing from niches and fissures where lichen by-products and other debris has

Alumroot

accumulated from run-off.

In the Northern Rockies Alumroot can be found at elevations as low as 3500', but it is generally found much higher in areas of more moderate climate, sometimes as high as 9000'. Wet, shady, rocky banks and slopes are always the first place to look for this plant.

ACTIONS
One of nature's astringent heavyweights, Alumroot can contain up to 20% tannins. It is effective in stimulating the healing of gastric disorders.

PROPAGATION & GROWTH CHARACTERISTICS
The nature of this plant's habitat allows the plant to reseed itself largely by mere coincidence. Seeds are very small and need light to break dormancy. If seeds do not find their way into the same nook as the parent plant, they are usually carried downslope by gravity or run-off. The seeds must then happen upon a spot where they can receive the correct amounts of light, water, and soil structure in order to germinate and take root... poor odds indeed for a seed that is smaller than a pinhead!

According to Janice J. Schofield, author of *Discovering Wild Plants,* the crown of the plant can be successfully transplanted if only the lower section of root is harvested.

GATHERING SEASON AND GENERAL GUIDELINES
Collect the root after the plant has dropped its seeds (June to September)..

Although late-season roots generally contain higher concentrations of active constituents (tannins), Alumroot should be gathered as early as possible after it has dropped its seeds. This allows more time for transplanted crowns to take root before winter. To assure the highest degree of transplant success, plant the crowns in exactly the same spot from which they were removed.

Alumroot

Heuchera species

Alumroot

PARTS USED
The root.

CARE AFTER GATHERING
Like all roots that are gathered from a damp environment, Alumroot is susceptible to mold if not given dry, well ventilated drying conditions. If roots are large, cut them in half lengthwise and spread them loosely on a non-metallic drying rack or a clean piece of paper. After the root is dried it can be ground into powder and stored in an airtight jar for future use. Be sure that your storage container is non-metallic and is away from sunlight.
The root can be tinctured fresh or dry for indefinite shelf life. FRESH ROOT: 1:2 Ratio, 50% alc. & 10% glycerine; DRIED ROOT: 1:5 Ratio, 50% alc. & 10% glycerine·
The dried, powdered root is an excellent styptic powder for shaving nicks, etc.

COMMON COMPANION HERBS
Although Alumroot is often found standing alone, you may find *Catspaw, Uva-ursi,* and *Valerian* keeping it company.

PLANT/ANIMAL INTERDEPENDENCE
In instances where Alumroot grows from fissures in rocky cliffs it creates a microcosm of minute organisms. These vertical mini-habitats are very delicate and serve critical roles in maintaining life in an otherwise uninhabitable environment.
The proportionately extensive roots of this plant often serve a critical; sometimes exclusive role as an erosion control agent. The EcoHerbalist needs to take into full account the fragile balances this plant maintains within its ecosystem.

IMPACT CONSIDERATIONS
Alumroot often lives in an environment that is well suited to mountain goats; not people. For the sake of habitat,

Alumroot

please avoid vertical adventures and gather Alumroot from areas with easy access and solid footing (for humans). If you feel that you *must* gather roots from a steep slope, wear proper footwear and maneuver slowly and cautiously to avoid unnecessary slipping and sliding. Moving a single rock or dislodging a tuft of moss could compromise next year's growth. Plan your approach carefully. Monitor the effects of your gathering and transplant efforts closely... in any case.

PHOTO REFERENCES
Discovering Wild Plants, Alaska, Canada, The Northwest, Janice J. Schofield (also technical information)
The Audubon Society Field Guide to North American Wildflowers, Richard Spellenberg

TECHNICAL REFERENCES
Medicinal Plants of the Pacific West, Michael Moore
Edible and Medicinal Plants of the Rocky Mountains and Neighbouring Territories, Terry Willard, Ph.D. (also has photo)
Quick Reference to Medicinal Plants of the Northern Rockies, Mary Wulff-Tilford

Alumroot

STAND LOCATIONS

Date of Discovery	Location and Description of Stand	Site Record #

Field Notes

Angelica

Angelica spp. Umbelliferae

IMPACT LEVEL: 2

DESCRIPTION

A hollow stemmed plant, 2'-5' high when mature. The large leaves are divided into what appear as opposite, individual ones, each about 2" long. Leaf surfaces are smooth or lightly hairy on their undersides, and are oval to lance-shaped with serrated edges.

The leaf veins of Angelica terminate at the tips of the serrations *(4.1)*, unlike those of the very poisonous *Water Hemlock,* which has leaf veins terminating at the bottom of the leaf serrations *(4.2)*.

Stems are often purple or reddish at the base, but not always.

The odor of this plant is similar to the odor of Lovage, but with a conifer overtone. It is an odor that becomes very distinctive as you gain familiarity with the plant, and is useful in distinguishing it from poisonous look-alikes.

Like other members of the Umbelliferae family, the flowers of Angelica are umbel-shaped, and are well described as looking like a fireworks burst. The umbels consist of hundreds of tiny, white flowers, which later develop into **white to very light brown, double-sided seeds that are reminiscent of angel wings, a characteristic that makes this plant easily distinguishable from Water Hemlock.** Water Hemlock has small, corky, somewhat kidney-shaped seeds that are very different from those of Angelica.

The root of Angelica is large and fleshy, medium-brown, and distinctively tapered. **The inside of the root is solid. Cut the root in half, lengthwise. If the interior is**

39

Angelica

chambered, you may have gathered the root of Water Hemlock. This is not a conclusive way to identify Water Hemlock though, as it does not always have chambered roots. One should also take note that cross breeding between Angelica and Water Hemlock may occur. Examine your stand carefully for Water Hemlock before gathering Angelica. If Water Hemlock is present, don't gather Angelica! Several species of Angelica exist in North America. All are useful...check your local references for the varieties in your area.

Angelica spp.

Angelica

*Fig. 4.1 The leaf veins of Angelica species terminate at the **tips of the margins**, unlike its poisonous relative, Water Hemlock (Cicuta douglasii). See Fig. 4.2.*

HABITAT

Angelica is generally found very close to water, but usually not standing in it. It prefers the fringes of wet, boggy areas, and is common along stream banks, springs, and roadside ditches.

Angelica can be found growing in any degree of sun exposure, but it seems to prefer a 50/50 mix of sun and shade.

Angelica

Fig. 4.2 Water Hemlock is **very poisonous** and looks similar to Angelica species. However, the leaf veins of Water Hemlock terminate at the **bottom of the leaf margin notches**. This particular specimen of Cicuta spp. has leaves that are sharply lanceolate. The leaves of this poisonous look-alike are often much broader.

ACTIONS
Antispasmodic, carminative, expectorant, diaphoretic, diuretic. An effective astringent to the stomach lining and a menstrual stimulant that helps to reduce cramps.

Angelica

PROPAGATION & GROWTH CHARACTERISTICS

Angelica is a perennial that may require two seasons or more to produce viable seeds. Seeds are distributed by alluvial action and by animals. Seeds require cold stratification in order to germinate.

The plant likes rich, moist soils that range from slightly alkaline to slightly acidic, depending on the species.

Angelica can be found from seashore to montaine forests below 8000'. It is easily grown in the garden... which I strongly recommend if you are less than certain in the identification of this plant.

GATHERING SEASON AND GENERAL GUIDELINES

Gather Angelica as late in the season as possible; late summer to early fall, after the seeds have ripened and have started to fall off. Do not wait too long, as positive identification becomes difficult after the seeds are completely gone. Since the root is generally the only part used, leave the upper parts where the plant was dug to decompose. Mature roots are often more than two years old, so careful impact monitoring and the use of multiple gathering sites is necessary. Pre-examination of the root maturity can be accomplished by carefully removing soil away from the base of the plant. If the taproot is small, let the plant grow and move on to another.

PARTS USED

The root.

CARE AFTER GATHERING

Cut the roots lengthwise and allow to dry it in a well-ventilated, dark location. The use of fresh root is not recommended. Tincture DRIED ROOT: 1:5 Ratio, 50%–65% alcohol.

COMMON COMPANION HERBS

Angelica is often found growing within a dense

Angelica

entanglement of other plants. Some of these companions may include *Horsetail, Stinging Nettle, False Solomon's Seal, Cleavers, Mints,* and very frequently *Cow Parsnip.*

PLANT/ANIMAL INTERDEPENDENCE
Angelica provides habitat for ground-nesting birds and small mammals, and concealment for the tired deer, elk, moose and bear.
The plant is an effective pollinator-attractor and should be left undisturbed during its bloom period.
The juicy, green foliage composts quickly after die-off and contributes substantially to the soil structure of its environment.

IMPACT CONSIDERATIONS
The moist, riparian soils in which Angelica resides are easily compacted and often host to a dense proliferation of other plant growth. Wading through such stands of vegetation requires careful and sometimes meticulous maneuvering to avoid damage to foliage and root systems. One must also take into account the possible presence of animals, insects, and their dwellings. Angelica is a common plant... find a stand that is easily accessed with minimal soil compaction.

PHOTO REFERENCES
The New Age Herbalist, Richard Mabey
Medicinal Plants, Peterson Field Guides, Foster & Duke
Discovering Wild Plants, Janice J. Schofield

TECHNICAL REFERENCES
Medicinal Plants of the Pacific West, Michael Moore
The Holistic Herbal, David Hoffmann
Herbal Healing for Women, Rosemary Gladstar
Weeds of the West, The Western Society of Weed Science (contains good photos of Water Hemlock)

Angelica

Vascular Plants of West-Central Montana, Klaus Lackschewitz
The Male Herbal, James Green
The Herb Book, John Lust
Quick Reference to Medicinal Plants of the Northern Rockies, Mary Wulff-Tilford

STAND LOCATIONS

Date of Discovery	Location and Description of Stand	Site Record #

Arnica

Arnica spp.   Compositae

IMPACT LEVEL: 2

OTHER NAMES
Leopard's Bane, Wolf's Bane.

DESCRIPTION
A perennial, Arnica is one of the first spring flowers to emerge here in Montana. Flowers are bright yellow and look like a small sunflower; about the size of a daisy (2"-3½" wide). Each plant has one to three flower heads when mature. Two to four pairs of 1½" -5" long leaves grow alternately beneath the flowers.

The leaves range from lance-shaped to a nearly circular heart shape. Most species have toothed leaf margins, and some have leaves that are 1-3 times as wide as they are long. Stems and leaves are smooth to moderately hairy and are generally very pungent, with a strong sage-pine odor.

Some varieties of Arnica, such as *A. parryi,* produce flowers that are completely absent of rays, which gives them a plucked appearance. All species are small plants, seldom more than 20" tall, with the majority of the species under 10". Arnica is often found in large, dense patches.

HABITAT
Arnica is a mountain plant that grows in partially shaded meadows, hillsides, and wooded areas from about 3500' to well above timberline. It loves soils that are rich in organic matter, especially conifer debris, and is often found growing from the thick mats of needles beneath pines, firs, and spruces.

Arnica

Arnica has a rather short bloom period and may not bloom at all during drought conditions.

Arnica spp.

ACTIONS
Anti-inflammatory and vulnerary. Arnica is very useful as a topical preparation for bruises, sprains, **and other closed injuries.** **Do not use internally.**

PROPAGATION & GROWTH CHARACTERISTICS
Arnica is a perennial that blooms during its second year and every year thereafter. It is commonly found growing in dense colonies where a single rhizome may extend beneath the

Arnica

surface of forest duff for several feet, sending up a proliferation of offshoots.

Arnica reseeds itself effectively after it has reached maturity. Seeds can be started in moist, light sand or root cuttings can be transplanted directly into the garden. When introducing Arnica into the herb garden, try to duplicate the specific habitat from which each plant was removed, and beware of its tendency to spread.

GATHERING SEASON AND GENERAL GUIDELINES

The best time to collect Arnica is at the beginning of its bloom period, when flowers are just starting to open (May-late July). Since this plant may take two years or more to bloom non-flowering plants should be left to grow. Although the flowers are generally recognized by herbalists as the most desirable part, the entire aerial plant contains the constituents needed for medicinal use. Bearing this in mind, I like to gather this plant after its bloom cycle (whenever possible) to allow for natural reseeding.

When gathering Arnica, grasp the plant at the base of its stem, just below ground level. Snap the upper plant off, leaving the rhizomes behind for perennial growth. Wear gloves, as the volatile oils of this herb can be absorbed through the skin.

PARTS USED

All aerial (above ground) parts.

CARE AFTER GATHERING

After gathering Arnica during its bloom period one begins to wonder what the purpose is in picking the flowers. Regardless of how tight the buds may be, you will likely return home with a bag of white and yellow fluff. This appears to be a survival mechanism, as the fluff contains viable seed... regardless of the cyclic interruption.

This herb is best if used fresh. Arnica oil can be made in the field by cutting up the herb and placing it in a jar as you

Arnica

harvest, then covering the herb with olive oil. The oil should be covered and kept away from light for one month, after which it is strained and stored.

The plant can be tinctured fresh or dried (fresh is best), **for topical use only.** TINCTURE FRESH PLANT: 1:2 Ratio; DRIED PLANT: 1:5 Ratio in 70% alcohol.

COMMON COMPANION HERBS
Oregon Grape, Valerian, False Solomon's Seal, Uva-ursi are but a few of Arnica's close neighbors.

PLANT/ANIMAL INTERDEPENDENCE
Arnica is an effective and important pollinator-attractor within its habitat. It is host to a wide variety of insects that play integral roles within the ecosystem. The plant's extensive rhizomes aerate the forest floor and provide habitat for subterranean insects, rodents, and other creatures.

IMPACT CONSIDERATIONS
In areas where Arnica grows through thick mats of forest debris, soil compaction can be a problem. These areas should not be walked upon immediately following periods of precipitation. High-compost soils lose resiliency when wet, so gather Arnica during dry weather, when the forest floor feels springy beneath your feet. Do not collect Arnica during drought or dormant periods when blooming does not occur, as the maturity of the plant is difficult to determine during these times.

PHOTO REFERENCES
The Audubon Society Field Guide to North American Wildflowers, Richard Spellenberg
Discovering Wild Plants, Alaska, Western Canada, the Northwest, Janice J. Schofield
The New Age Herbalist, Richard Mabey

Arnica

TECHNICAL REFERENCES
The Holistic Herbal, David Hoffmann
Medicinal Plants of the Pacific West, Michael Moore
Vascular Plants of Montana, Dorn
The Male Herbal, James Green

STAND LOCATIONS

Date of Discovery	Location and Description of Stand	Site Record #

Balsamroot

Balsamorrhiza sagittata   Compositae

IMPACT LEVEL: 2

OTHER NAMES
Arrowleaf Balsamroot.

DESCRIPTION
Balsamroot has large (3"-5") bright yellow flowers that distinguish them as obvious members of the Sunflower family. The often profuse display of flowers are on individual, leafless stalks that grow above the basal cluster of leaves.

Leaves are large, often reaching a foot in length, and are distinctively arrow-shaped. The plant is covered with velvet-like hairs that give the leaves a silvery-gray appearance.

Balsamroot blooms in early to mid-spring and is often the first yellow flower to appear in its habitat. It has a long bloom period, and is often the *last* yellow flower left standing in late summer.

Roots are thick and tapered, and sometimes weigh three pounds or more when mature. Mature roots are often very woody and tough, with taproots that can extend two feet into hardpan subsoils. The roots are very resinous, and have a rich, pine-like odor.

HABITAT
Balsamroot flourishes on dry, open hillsides with southern to western sun exposure. It is well adapted to shallow, rocky soils that are low in organic matter, and often appears alone on otherwise blank hillsides.

Although found at higher elevations, it is most commonly found in the 3000' to 7000' range.

Balsamroot

ACTIONS
Antimicrobial, expectorant, disinfectant, immuno-stimulant. Although not as potent, Balsamroot serves as an excellent alternative to *Echinacea*, a popular herb that is currently being wiped out by over-harvest, commercial greed, and habitat destruction.

PROPAGATION & GROWTH CHARACTERISTICS
A perennial, Balsamroot is a hardy, drought tolerant plant that grows very slowly. Although it reseeds itself readily, a large mature root can be over ten years old.

The transplant of whole roots is generally impossible with older plants because of the extensive taproot, but successful transplant of root crowns is possible. After digging the root, pull the crowns laterally away from the root as carefully as possible and transplant into the same area from which it was gathered... or introduce it into the herb garden.

Seeds require stratification in order to germinate, and are naturally distributed by animals or spring run-off.

GATHERING SEASON AND GENERAL GUIDELINES
Gather the roots anytime after the plant blooms and has gone to seed... usually late-July to late-August. If you wait too long the roots become very dry and woody, making processing procedures very difficult and reducing the quality of your finished product.

PARTS USED
The root.

CARE AFTER GATHERING
Since this plant is a slow grower and the mature roots are generally very large, it is a good idea to plan on tincturing the fresh root for long term storage. One root can easily supply a household with tincture for several years, and by making a tincture right away you can eliminate any risk of spoilage or loss of constituents through drying. Cut the roots

Balsamroot

on a board that you plan to use exclusively for herbs, because the sticky resins will get all over it. Cut the roots into small chunks (1" or less), and TINCTURE FRESH ROOT: 1:2 Ratio; 70% alcohol.

If you *must* dry the roots, cut them lengthwise two or three times and stack them loosely in a paper bag. Then TINCTURE THE DRY ROOT: 1:5 ratio; 70% alcohol or use in teas or decoctions. The dried root will keep for 6-12 months if stored in airtight glass jars, away from sunlight.

COMMON COMPANION HERBS

Lomatium, Mullein, Yarrow, Uva-ursi, and *Oregon Grape* are a few.

PLANT/ANIMAL INTERDEPENDENCE

Where Balsamroot grows on steep, sparsely vegetated hillsides it plays an important role in protecting against erosion. The large roots hold shallow soil in place to support the presence of grasses and other important wildlife forage.

The large, heat-resistant leaves provide food and shelter for a multitude of insects and small animals, and are sometimes browsed upon by deer and elk as well. I have seen evidence of bears digging the roots shortly after their winter nap.

The large yellow flowers are effective pollinator-attractors, and serve a critical roll among their less conspicuous plant companions.

The large basal leaves provide precious compost to otherwise deleted soils after they die back in the fall.

IMPACT CONSIDERATIONS

The EcoHerbalist must remember that Balsamroot is a very slow grower, and must be aware of the the long-term absence of the plant after harvest. Vicarious impacts such as erosion, loss of interdependent forage, and reduction of small animal shelter must be taken into full account prior to gathering, especially in areas where Balsamroot stands as the

53

Balsamroot

primary plant in its habitat. Hillside habitats should be monitored closely, particularly throughout the spring melt and rainy seasons. In areas where erosion is already occurring or impact by animals is high, Balsamroot should be left to do its job at hillside maintenance. Examples of such areas include those that are grazed by livestock or areas that are frequented by large herds of deer or elk that have been concentrated into a limited range because of urban pressures.

In all cases it is best to gather from a healthy stand of plants on relatively level terrain.

PHOTO REFERENCES
The Audubon Society Field Guide to North American Wildflowers, Richard Spellenberg

Nature Bound Pocket Field Guide (photo and info. on *B. deltoidea* variety), Ron Dawson

TECHNICAL REFERENCES
Edible and Medicinal Plants of the Northern Rockies and Neighbouring Territories, Terry Willard, Ph.D. (this book also contains a good photo)
Medicinal Plants of the Pacific West, Michael Moore

Although this plant has a long Native American history as food and medicine, relatively little information has been published about its medicinal qualities.

Balsamroot

STAND LOCATIONS

Date of Discovery	Location and Description of Stand	Site Record #

Field Notes

Bee Balm

Monarda fistulosa   Lamiaceae

IMPACT LEVEL 2

OTHER NAMES
Wild Bergamot, Purple Bee Balm, Horsemint, Wild Oregano, Oswego Tea.

DESCRIPTION
A very pungent plant, Bee Balm is very similar in odor and appearance to culinary varieties of Oregano. Leaves are lance-shaped, simple, opposite, and have a tendency of curving backward toward the ground. Leaf margins are sometimes, but not always toothed. Like most members of the Mint family, the stems of Bee Balm are distinctively square. Flowers are presented in 1"-3" terminal clusters, each containing dozens of tiny, rose to purple-colored blossoms. The plant can grow to 3', but is generally found in the 6"-18" range.

HABITAT
Bee Balm likes meadows and slopes that are predominantly dry and sunny. Like most Mints, this plant is adaptable to a wide variety of soils. *Unlike* most Mints, Bee Balm is very drought-tolerant, and prefers dryland habitats.
Bee Balm (*Monarda fistulosa)* is generally found at elevations below 4000'. Other varieties of *Monarda,* such as *M. methaefolia,* grow at higher elevation in shady, moist soils.
The range of this plant remains largely undefined, but it seems to be spreading westward from the eastern United States. Livestock enjoy grazing upon this plant, and have

Bee Balm

undoubtedly served as a vehicle in the expansion of Bee Balm's range.

ACTIONS
Diaphoretic, carminative, antiseptic, and anesthetic. Bee Balm is particularly useful as a sore throat remedy.

PROPAGATION & GROWTH CHARACTERISTICS
Bee Balm is a perennial that reseeds itself readily and transplants well. Other varieties of *Monarda* are difficult to start from seed, whereas *M.fistulosa* is not. This is an excellent plant to introduce into your herb garden. No stratification or other special treatment is required, and it is adaptable to just about any soil.

GATHERING SEASON AND GENERAL GUIDELINES
Gather the leaves when the plant is in bloom (May-Sept., depending on location)...this is when they are strongest. Pluck individual leaves to minimize impact, or gather the stem and leaves after the plant has bloomed and gone to seed. If the latter is your choice, clip the stems about 1" above ground level to allow for perennial regrowth and root protection. When gathering while the plant is in bloom, always be sure to leave plenty of flowers intact for pollination and seed development.

PARTS USED
Leaves if plucked from the plant; the entire aerial plant if stem is taken.

CARE AFTER GATHERING
This herb is generally used as an infusion for sore throats. Dry the leaves and/or the aerial parts in a dry, well-ventilated area that is away from light. Although the fresh plant can be used, the herb tastes much more pleasant when dried. The dried herb will only keep in quality condition for six months or so if properly stored in airtight containers, so

Bee Balm

be conservative when collecting.

COMMON COMPANION HERBS

Although there are too many to list, *St. John's wort*, *Burdock*, *Arnica*, *Balsamroot*, *Dandelion*, and *Valerian* are a few common neighbors.

PLANT/ANIMAL INTERDEPENDENCE

As it's name implies, Bee Balm is very attractive to bees and other pollinators. This natural attribute not only serves a reproductive function for Bee Balm itself, but attracts beneficial insects to surrounding plants as well. Bee Balm is foraged upon by a wide variety of wildlife, so carefully assess the quality and quantity of other forages in an area before you begin gathering. If the presence of grasses and other forage is scarce, leave the Bee Balm for our animal companions.

IMPACT CONSIDERATIONS

Bee Balm is often found in abundance in areas that are grazed by livestock. Beware of the possible presence of herbicides in these areas, particularly if you notice the presence of what your agricultural community may recognize as "noxious weeds". It is wise to check with your local authorities prior to gathering herbs from these areas. When gathering from grazed areas it is also important to take a good look at the severity of impact that is being caused by the livestock. If possible, try to determine just how many cows, horses, sheep, etc. are using the area to develop an estimate of how much of the plant life remains vulnerable in the near future. Watch the area for several days before wildcrafting... you may be surprised (and/or disgusted). Here in Western Montana it is fairly common to find a dense stand of plants one day, only to find the same stand completely devoured or trampled by cattle the next. In any case, it is always desirable to gather Bee Balm from low impact areas.

Bee Balm

PHOTO REFERENCES
Peterson Field Guides, Eastern/Central Medicinal Plants, Foster & Duke
The Beaudoin Easy Method of Identifying Wildflowers, Viola Kneeland Beaudoin

TECHNICAL REFERENCES
Vascular Plants of Montana, Dorn
Medicinal Plants of the Mountain West, Michael Moore
Edible and Medicinal Plants of the Rocky Mountains and Neighbouring Territories, Terry Willard, Ph.D. (also has a good photo)
Quick Reference to Medicinal Plants of the Northern Rockies, Mary Wulff-Tilford

STAND LOCATIONS

Date of Discovery	Location and Description of Stand	Site Record #

Burdock

Arctium spp.   Compositae/Asteraceae

IMPACT LEVEL: 1

OTHER NAMES
>Clotbur, Lappa.

DESCRIPTION
>A biennial, Burdock first emerges as a rosette of large, irregular, basal leaves. The second year produces a thick, heavily leaved stalk that can grow to 10' high. Leaves grow alternately from the erect stalk, which later develops alternate, leaf-bearing branches. The large 3"-12" wide basal leaves of the mature plant are generally heart-shaped. The upper leaves are smaller, and vary in shape to nearly oval. The lower surfaces of all leaves are paler in color than the upper surfaces.
>**The entire plant is covered with fine hairs that make the plant feel sticky-abrasive... like extra-fine grit sandpaper.**
>The **terminate flowers** are purple in color and are somewhat inconspicuous, except for their bristly, thistle-like burrs. Each burr is equipped with a multitude of backward-hooked spines that attach to anything that brushes against them. After the plant matures and dries the burrs harden, making their hooks even more effective. **Dark, shiny seeds are contained within each burr.**
>The root is large (often huge), tapered, and slightly aromatic. A shovel, digging bar, and axe are sometimes needed to extricate the root, which can be three feet in length and weigh several pounds. Burdock is often confused with its relative, Cocklebur (*Xanthium strumarium*). The identifying differences between the two plants are in the characteristics of

Burdock

their burrs.　**On Burdock, the burrs grow from stem tips,
whereas Cocklebur has its burrs alongside the stems.　Also,
the burrs of Burdock contain several dark-colored seeds,
whereas the burrs of Cocklebur contain two, flat seeds that
look somewhat like sunflower seeds.**

HABITAT

Burdock grows in disturbed areas, such as roadsides,
landfills, irrigation ditches, and alluvial accumulations.　It
grows sporadically at lower elevations (usually below 5000')
throughout North America.

ACTIONS

Alterative, diuretic and bitter.　Burdock is well known
as a blood purifier.

PROPAGATION & GROWTH CHARACTERISTICS

Burdock remains inconspicuous during its first year,
then reaches for the sky during its second.　After blooming,
the plant dies... leaving behind thousands of seeds to be
distributed by anything that walks too close.　It is a *very*
successful survivalist.　Burdock was introduced from Eurasia,
where it is still marketed as a vegetable.　Although it was
likely introduced into North America for the same purpose, it
is now regarded by many as a troublesome weed that invades
pastures, fields, and waste areas.　In Western Montana
Burdock grows in areas where it has been introduced mainly
by livestock.　Once this plant is established it is likely to
proliferate.　It prefers sunny locations with rich soil and plenty
of moisture, but will grow with some success under almost any
conditions.

GATHERING SEASON AND GENERAL GUIDELINES

Although the root is a useable medicine at anytime, fall
harvest of first year growth is recommended.　This is partly
because of the plant's taproot...digging a mature root can be
like excavating a small phone pole.　Another consideration is

Burdock

the burr factor. *They will cover you!* If you don't mind the burr attack, be sure you have removed all of the little beasties from your clothing, hair, and orifices (nude gathering *is not* recommended) before travelling elsewhere... Burdock can be very intrusive to the unaccustomed ecosystem. If you are collecting the roots to eat, young first year plants are best. Burdock is easy to grow in the garden, but it is wise to pull the plants the first year to avoid herbal mutiny.

PARTS USED
Primarily the root, although seeds are sometimes tinctured as well.

CARE AFTER GATHERING
The root can be used fresh or dried, but as a general rule we like to use the root fresh. This eliminates shelf life problems and the loss of active constituents. Roots should be cut lengthwise, then crosswise into manageable pieces before drying, tincturing, or use in infusions. Dry the roots with plenty of ventilation. TINCTURE: FRESH ROOT, 1:2 Ratio; DRIED ROOT, 1:5 Ratio; 50% alcohol. SEED TINCTURE: 1:5/50% alcohol.

COMMON COMPANION HERBS
Nettle, Dock, Cleavers, Catnip, Horsetail, St. John's Wort, Dandelion, Arnica, Angelica, and *Bee Balm* are often found nearby.

PLANT/ANIMAL INTERDEPENDENCE
Although Burdock is an alien that has altered the ecosystems in which it chooses to live, it does offer some benefits to its adopted neighborhoods. Burdock's massive roots are effective in reducing erosion in high-impact areas. The plant's abundant foliage provides food and shelter for birds and small animals in areas where habitat may have been damaged by human activities (such as free-ranging livestock or excavation). When the plant's juicy leaves die back they

Burdock

contribute considerable amounts of rich compost to the soil. The plant is entirely edible to humans and many animals, and is readily foraged upon during periods when other food plants have been depleted.

Burdock is a plant that grows in areas subject to human impact, and it possesses a rather unique characteristic of remaining within the vicinity of where it was originally introduced. It is very common to find a large population of Burdock in one area, and a total absence of it in the surrounding fifty mile radius. Given this characteristic and the nature of its chosen habitat, perhaps Burdock is designed by Nature to help restore balance in areas that we humans have selfishly damaged.

IMPACT CONSIDERATIONS

In view of Burdock's aggressive growth characteristics, the wildcrafter must take into account its ability to restructure an ecosystem... beneficially or otherwise. The longer it has been within a particular ecosystem, the more defined its role becomes. As natural caretakers it is important to recognize, respect, and understand symbiotic relationships. We must re-think the collective attitude that places Burdock in the category of "troublesome weeds". It is important to be aware of the possible consequences which may result if we introduce plants like Burdock into new areas. Burdock is an easy plant for the EcoHerbalist to monitor, but special care is necessary to prevent introduction of this plant into pristine areas.

PHOTO REFERENCES

Weeds of the West, The Western Society of Weed Science
Northwest Weeds, Ronald J. Taylor

TECHNICAL REFERENCES

Wise Woman Herbal - Healing Wise, Susun S. Weed
Medicinal Plants of the Mountain West, Michael Moore

Burdock

Peterson Field Guide - Eastern/Central Medicinal Plants, Foster & Duke
The Holistic Herbal, David Hoffmann
The Healing Herbs, Michael Castleman
Quick Reference - Medicinal Plants of the Northern Rockies, Mary Wulff-Tilford
The Herb Book, John Lust

STAND LOCATIONS

Date of Discovery	Location and Description of Stand	Site Record #

Catnip

Nepeta cataria   Lamiaceae

IMPACT LEVEL: 2

OTHER NAMES
Catmint.

DESCRIPTION
Catnip is distinctively a mint, with square stems and opposing leaves. The entire plant is covered with soft, velvet-like hair that gives the plant a blue-gray appearance. Leaves are ovate, ½"-2" wide, with distinctively round-toothed margins. Flowers are white with purplish-pink spots, ¼"-½" long, tubular in shape, blooming in terminal clusters. Wild Catnip is very aromatic and is usually much stronger than commercially grown and dried feline entertainment products. The fresh plant has a strong, skunky-mint odor that demands recognition, and is very different from the stale, dried product found in the pet store. Plants range from 6" to 5' when mature, depending on growing conditions.

HABITAT
Catnip was introduced from Europe at the time of the earliest Anglo colonizations. It was considered a cure-all, and has been distributed to just about every part of the globe that was explored by the Europeans. It prefers sunny, moist disturbed areas, and is frequently found along roadsides, irrigation ditches, pastures, and rangelands throughout North America. Although it is adaptable to just about any elevation, it appears to be most abundant within the 3000'-5000' range here in the Mountain Northwest.

Catnip

ACTIONS
Mild sedative, antispasmodic, diaphoretic.

PROPAGATION & GROWTH CHARACTERISTICS
Catnip is a perennial that likes rich, slightly acid and well-drained soils, full sun, and plenty of moisture. It can be propagated from seed, but is easier to establish from transplants or root cuttings. Catnip is a hardy plant; adaptable to Zone 3, and is commercially grown with great success as far north as Alaska. Although an alien, Catnip is not highly competitive with other plants. It is an excellent choice for the home herb garden.

GATHERING SEASON & GENERAL GUIDELINES
Gather Catnip just as it is beginning to bloom, generally in mid-summer. Collect the lower leaves for minimum impact, or clip stems. If you choose to gather the stems and upper plant, cut the stem six inches or more above the ground to protect the roots and allow perennial growth. Be sure to leave plenty of flowers for pollination and seed distribution.

PARTS USED
The leaves, or the entire upper plant if stems were cut.

CARE AFTER GATHERING
Dry the herb as soon as possible in a warm, dry, well-ventilated area on a non-metallic screen or cheesecloth. Keep away from sunlight and toss the herb frequently while drying to expedite the process and avoid mold. Dried Catnip is used primarily in tea, and is a very pleasant one at that. The fresh plant, although useful, tends to be strong and bitter-tasting.

COMMON COMPANION HERBS
Stinging Nettle, Burdock, Angelica, Cleavers, Self Heal, Pyrola, and other members of the Mint family often share habitat with Catnip.

Catnip

PLANT/ANIMAL INTERDEPENDENCE

Catnip often grows in thick, bushy stands that provide habitat for birds, amphibians, and reptiles. It is an effective pollinator-attractor, and is host to a multitude of insects and spiders. I have witnessed the consumption of Catnip by birds and the occasional deer, but it is certainly not high on the herbivore shopping list. Mountain lions, lynx, and bobcats occasionally cut-loose and partake in the plant's feline-narcotic qualities, but not to the extent that the wildcrafter need worry about stumbling over a big, tripped-out puss.

IMPACT CONSIDERATIONS

Catnip often grows in soils that compress easily, so wear soft footwear and gather the herb during dry periods (but not drought). Catnip often grows within a proliferation of other plants, so careful maneuvering is necessary to prevent vicarious damage. Try to gather from the periphery of large patches, bearing in mind that removal of too much vegetation may compromise small animal and insect habitat... a visual difference in the stand following harvest is indicative of taking too much. If you are gathering within grazed or other "managed" areas, be aware of the possible presence of herbicides, especially if "noxious weeds" are present.

PHOTO REFERENCES

Peterson Field Guides, Eastern/Central Medicinal Plants, Foster & Duke
The Healing Herbs, Michael Castleman

TECHNICAL REFERENCES

Medicinal Plants of the Mountain West, Michael Moore
Rodale's Illustrated Encyclopedia of Herbs, Rodale
The Holistic Herbal, David Hoffmann
Quick Reference - Medicinal Plants of the Northern Rockies, Mary Wulff-Tilford

Catnip

STAND LOCATIONS

Date of Discovery	Location and Description of Stand	Site Record #

Field Notes

Cat's Paw

Antennaria spp.   Compositae (Asteraceae)

Impact Level: 2

OTHER NAMES
Pussy-toes, Life Everlasting.

DESCRIPTION
This large genus is characterized by its **little cluster of small, ball-shaped, rayless, flowers that resemble the toe pattern of a cat's foot.** The multi-flowered terminal clusters range in color from snow-white to pink. The leaves are small (under 1") in most   species, and are lanceolate. **The entire plant is covered with a white fuzz that gives the plant a silvery appearance.** The plants often form dense, silvery-gray mats on the forest floor. **All *antennarias* have rhizomatous roots... if you pull a plant and it has a taproot, then it is not Cat's Paw.**

Of the dozen or more varieties that grow in the Mountain West, few are taller than 6" when fully mature.

HABITAT
Cat's Paw is found in dry, often rocky montaine forest clearings.   It is most abundant   within the 6000'-9000' elevation range, and is frequently found as dense mats in larch and lodgepole forests.

ACTIONS
Anti-inflammatory to the liver and astringent to the intestinal tract.

Cat's Paw

PROPAGATION & GROWTH CHARACTERISTICS

Cat's Paw is a perennial that can be found in full shade but prefers at least 3 or 4 hours of sunlight each day. Many varieties of this species are reproductively self-sufficient and do not require pollination to produce viable seeds. The seeds are very, *very* small and require cold-stratification to break dormancy. Blooming occurs anytime from April to September, depending on the variety and the nature of its habitat.

GATHERING SEASON AND GENERAL GUIDELINES

Gather this plant as it begins to bloom...this is when the herb is most potent. When gathering from mat-like colonies pull the individual plants, as opposed to digging them. This alleviates unnecessary damage to the roots of the other plants. A visual impact upon the stand after harvest is indicative of gathering too much. Gather from the periphery of dense, healthy stands. Gather during dry weather to avoid spoilage and soil compaction.

PARTS USED

The entire plant.

CARE AFTER GATHERING

This herb is generally used fresh, in tea... so don't gather more than you can use within a week or so. The fresh plants can be refrigerated for a limited period before use, if kept dry.

COMMON COMPANION HERBS

Uva-ursi, Oregon Grape, Wild Strawberry, and *Arnica* are a few.

PLANT/ANIMAL INTERDEPENDENCE

Beneath dense mats of Cat's Paws lies a microcosm of insects and small mammals. These little islands of special habitat are particularly important at higher elevations or in rocky areas where cover is especially scarce for small prey

Cat's Paw

animals. As humans we tend to view creatures such as mice and voles as insignificant; even troublesome lower forms of life. But in the natural realm these animals play critical roles in maintaining plant and animal diversity... their absence from an ecosystem could mean the demise of dependent predators or the die-off of a plant that depends upon a rodent's seed distribution efforts.

The tight, colonial-growth characteristic of this plant is beneficial to the maintenance of soil structure. At high elevations in Montana I have observed the plant growing atop giant slabs of granite, where a 2" layer of soil is held in place almost exclusively by the plant's root systems and its protective ground cover.

IMPACT CONSIDERATIONS

As with all root/whole plant herbs, careful collection techniques and careful monitoring of the stand over a long period of time is essential to keep impact to a minimum. Try to gather this herb from areas where other growth and small animal cover is abundant. Learn which members of this large genus grows in your bioregion and try to focus on abundant varieties that grow independently. Avoid gathering from thick, colonial mats of Cat's Paw.

PHOTO REFERENCES

The Audubon Society Field Guide to North American Wildflowers, Richard Spellenberg

Forest Wildflowers, Dr. Dee Strickler

TECHNICAL REFERENCES

Peterson Field Guides Eastern/Central Medicinal Plants, Foster & Duke

Medicinal Plants of the Mountain West, Michael Moore

Quick Reference to Medicinal Plants of the Northern Rockies, Mary Wulff-Tilford

Cat's Paw

STAND LOCATIONS

Date of Discovery	Location and Description of Stand	Site Record #

Field Notes

Chickweed

Stellaria media   Caryophyllaceae

IMPACT LEVEL: 1

OTHER NAMES
Common Chickweed, Starweed.

DESCRIPTION
Chickweed is a sprawling weed that is often found growing in dense mats along streams, irrigation ditches, and pastures. Several varieties are widely distributed throughout North America.

The leaves of Chickweed are ovate to broadly lanceolate, up to 1½" in length, and grow opposite of one another.

Flowers are simple and white with five, two-parted petals that give each flower a ten-petal appearance. The flowers grow from leaf axils and at many of the numerous branch tips.

Stems have distinctive, minute hairs along one side of their length. Stems are weak and angular, with root nodes at various intervals that enable the plant to crawl about... much like strawberry runners. The entire plant has a sweet juiciness to it that makes it a delicious salad or sandwich participant.

HABITAT
If you haven't already found this plant, you just need to look harder. Chickweed was introduced into North America from Eurasia, and has since made itself at home from coast to coast. Its wide distribution in the U.S. is largely attributed to agricultural and landscaping activities. It is common to moist pastures, lawns, vacant lots, and roadside ditches. Some species can be found at high, subalpine elevations.

73

Chickweed

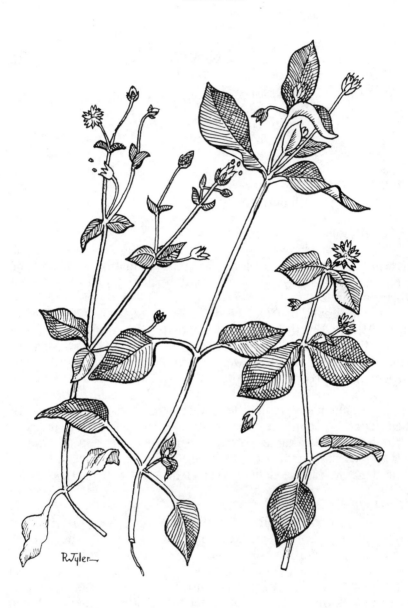

Stellaria media

Chickweed

ACTIONS

Externally it is an effective demulcent, and is useful for swelling conditions related to acute or chronic problems.

Internally it is a diuretic, and if eaten in *huge* quantities it acts as a laxative.

PROPAGATION & GROWTH CHARACTERISTICS

Most varieties are annuals, with a few perennial exceptions. In mountain climates the perennial varieties are often seen growing as annuals. It likes ample moisture and at least half a day of shade.

Chickweed is very good at reproducing. The plant crawls around, putting down roots along the way. To expedite its outward march, Chickweed continually blooms and produces seed throughout its growing season (which can be *all year* in mild climates). Some of the seed companies that are offering "gourmet salad greens" are selling Chickweed seed for the home garden. My crop was introduced to me in the form of horse manure. Although reproductively aggressive, Chickweed is not highly competitive with other plants and is easy to control in the garden through regular harvesting.

Although it can be grown in any soil, Chickweed prefers rich loam with a neutral to slightly acid pH. The soil must be consistently moist, but not boggy.

GATHERING SEASON AND GENERAL GUIDELINES

Chickweed can be gathered anytime. If you are gathering Chickweed for consumption in salads, etc., beware of plants that are wet and growing close to water... Chickweed has a reputation of harboring giardia and other nauseating microorganisms. Always wash the greens and allow them to dry off prior to eating them.

Despite its delicious flavor and medicinal qualities, Chickweed is considered a "noxious weed" in many locales. Be aware of the possible presence of herbicides, particularly in cultivated areas. Avoid gathering this plant from roadsides or city lots, where the plants tend to absorb airborne pollutants.

Chickweed

PARTS USED
The whole plant.

CARE AFTER GATHERING
This plant should be used fresh. It wilts and loses valuable constituents quickly, so it is best to make your tinctures and oils while in the field. The fresh herb is also useful and pleasant in tea.

TINCTURE FRESH HERB: 1:2 Ratio; 95% alcohol.

TO MAKE AN OIL: Stuff a glass jar with the cut up and wilted herb, cover with olive oil so that the herb is totally submerged. Seal the jar and store in a warm place for about one month. The oil is especially useful for itching and irritations.

COMMON COMPANION HERBS
Stinging Nettle, Angelica, Horsetail, Pyrola, Cleavers, and members of the Mint family are some common neighbors.

PLANT/ANIMAL INTERDEPENDENCE
Animals find Chickweed as delicious as we do. In areas where the plant dies back each fall, its green, juicy leaves and stems compost readily and are high in plant nutrients. The presence of Chickweed is generally indicative of rich soil.

IMPACT CONSIDERATIONS
Be careful to avoid the introduction of this plant into areas where it is not welcomed by herbicidal maniacs. Although Chickweed often proves beneficial to an ecosystem, this is not for us to decide. Leave Chickweed's distribution to the plant and its natural allies.

Stands that appear to be actively foraged upon should be left undisturbed. Our animal companions need the plants more than we do, and there is plenty of this abundant herb for all of us. Find a healthy stand that is easy to access with minimal subsequent impact. Soft, wet streambanks can and

Chickweed

should be avoided.

PHOTO REFERENCES
>*Weeds of the West,* Western Society of Weed Science
>*Northwest Weeds,* Ronald J. Taylor
>*The New Age Herbalist,* Richard Mabey
>*Nature Bound Pocket Field Guide,* Ron Dawson

TECHNICAL REFERENCES
>*Wise Woman Herbal - Healing Wise,* Susun S. Weed
>*Medicinal Plants of the Desert and Canyon West,* Michael Moore
>*Natural Healing with Herbs,* Humbart Santillo, BS, MH
>*Discovering Wild Plants,* Janice J. Schofield
>*The Holistic Herbal,* David Hoffmann
>*The Herb Book,* John Lust
>*Quick Reference - Medicinal Plants of the Northern Rockies,* Mary Wulff-Tilford

STAND LOCATIONS

Date of Discovery	Location and Description of Stand	Site Record #

Cleavers

Gallium spp.   Rubiaceae

Impact Level: 2

OTHER NAMES
Bedstraw, Catchweed, Goosegrass, Cleaver's Wort, Clivers.

DESCRIPTION
The *Gallium* species represents a large genus... (eight varieties are native to the Rocky Mountain region alone.) All are similar in appearance and growth characteristics. Generally speaking, *Galliums* have leaves that are narrow, ½"- 2" long, and grow in whorls of 4 to 8 that radiate from the stem in intervals... much like the spokes of a bicycle wheel. Stems are square. Flowers are tiny, white, and star shaped. The plant is delicately fragrant, with a sweet odor that made the species a popular bed stuffing through the turn of the century. Of the several varieties, *Gallium aparine* is the one most commonly used by herbalists, and is generally known as "Cleavers". Though all varieties of Gallium are medicinally useful, *G.aparine* has maintained popularity due to its **distinctive ability to cling to things... particularly clothing, in a fashion that is reminiscent of loose hair with a static charge.** This characteristic makes Cleavers easy to identify, and undoubtedly earned the plant its common name. Cleavers is a weak-stemmed plant that grows in tangled, climbing masses in moist, usually riparian areas. The plant has tiny, downward-pointing hooks along the angles of the stems that enable the plant to cling and climb. The hooks are easier felt than seen, making the stems feel sticky...especially when you run your fingers upward. The seed capsules of Cleavers present themselves as

Cleavers

pairs of little green balls that are well described by herbalist Michael Moore as "covered with little bristly hairs like green testicles". The favored status of *G.aparine* over other Galliums is unfortunate for the plant, as all varieties are useful, and many are ethically more desirable than *G.aparine* in terms of human impact. *Gallium aparine* is a delicate annual that chooses to grow in moist, easily compressed soils that are usually host to a thick profusion of other plants. Gathering Cleavers from this kind of habitat without damaging other plants is often difficult if not impossible. Other varieties, such as *Gallium boreale*, grow in drier, more stable soils. *G.boreale* is widely distributed throughout North America, and is very similar in appearance to Cleavers, except that it grows on **stout, self-supporting stems and does not have the clinging characteristic of *G. aparine*.** *G.boreale* is a perennial,(and is therefore much easier for the EcoHerbalist to monitor for regrowth and the effects of subsequent impact.)

HABITAT

Cleavers (*G.aparine*) can be found in moist, partially shaded areas, along streams and in wet draws, etc. It likes to climb, and is often found tangled within other plant growth. *Gallium boreale* (also known as Northern Bedstraw), is often seen growing alongside Cleavers, but it also frequents drier, sunny areas. It is a common resident of meadows and grassy roadsides. All of the *Galliums* like rich soil.

ACTIONS

Diuretic, anti-inflammatory, astringent, and lymphatic tonic. Cleavers and Northern Bedstraw are very gentle, good-tasting herbs. They are especially helpful in the healing of stomach ulcers, particularly if the juice of the plant is extracted and used in a pure, uncut form. Any number of commercially available juicers are suitable for the job.

Cleavers

Gallium species

Cleavers

PROPAGATION & GROWTH CHARACTERISTICS

Cleavers (*G.aparine*) is an annual. The plant has very delicate roots, does not transplant well, and is nearly impossible to start from seed. Northern Bedstraw (*G.boreale*) and many of the other perennial varieties are effective reproducers that are easy to establish from transplants or seeds. Stratification or other special treatments are unnecessary, and the plant can easily be introduced into the herb garden. All of the *Galliums* require consistently moist soils with neutral to slightly acid pH levels.

GATHERING SEASON AND GENERAL GUIDELINES

Gather *Galliums* during the early stages of their bloom period... generally sometime between mid-May and July. The annual Cleavers variety uproots easily, as its root system is much weaker than the stem. To allow for seed distribution, side stems of Cleavers can be snipped off, leaving the main stem and most of the flowers (and later the seeds) to reproduce. Otherwise, gather the entire plant and monitor your impact closely. Northern Bedstraw and other perennial varieties should be clipped off above ground level to allow for next year's growth. When clipping *Gallium boreale* take care not to compress soil at the base of the plant. Although it is desirable to gather herbs (particularly annuals) after they have bloomed and dropped their seeds, Cleavers often dies back immediately after blooming. However, in wet weather the plant tends to stand a little longer.

PARTS USED

All aerial parts

CARE AFTER GATHERING

Cleavers loses alot of its valuable protein constituents when it dries, so use the fresh plant or tincture the herb immediately. Have your tincturing jar and alcohol ready and with you when gathering the plant... cut it up and stuff it right into the jar with a 1:2 Ratio of 50% alcohol.

Cleavers

PLANT/ANIMAL INTERDEPENDENCE

Gallium tastes as sweet as it smells... it is relished by everything from field voles to the always-hungry moose. The tangle of vines that Cleavers creates is used by birds and small animals as a nesting material. In Western Montana, the absence of Cleavers at streamside is often indicative of a poor forage year, especially for animals that live exclusively within riparian habitats.

IMPACT CONSIDERATIONS

In case you haven't guessed, I see little or no reason to gather Cleavers (*G.aparine*) if other *Galliums* are present. If you *must* impact Cleavers' delicate habitat, be aware of vulnerable soil structure and the possible presence of bird nests and other dwellings. Move carefully and try not to damage other plants when removing a tangled clump of Cleavers. Wear soft footwear, tread lightly, and monitor your impacts closely for two or more years after gathering. Bear in mind that annuals must distribute seed each year to survive, and be very conservative in your collecting. **Gathering a quantity that effects the appearance of the stand *whatsoever* is indicative of over-harvest.**

PHOTO REFERENCES

Weeds of the West, The Wesern Society of Weed Science (has good photo of green testicles)

The Audubon Society Field Guide to North American Wildflowers, Richard Spellenberg

Forest Wildflowers, Dr. Dee Strickler

Northwest Weeds, Ronald J. Taylor

TECHNICAL REFERENCES

Discovering Wild Plants..., Janice J. Schofield

Medicinal Plants of the Mountain West, Michael Moore

The Holistic Herbal, David Hoffmann

Cleavers

STAND LOCATIONS

Date of Discovery	Location and Description of Stand	Site Record #

Field Notes

Clematis

Clematis spp.   Ranuculaceae

IMPACT LEVEL: 2

OTHER NAMES
Virgin's Bower, Old Man's Beard, Pepper Vine, Pipestems, Traveler's Joy.

DESCRIPTION
Several species of Clematis live in the Western United States, some quite different than others. Of the five species that grow in my area of Montana, I simply differentiate them as "the purple varieties" and the "cream-colored varieties". Of the three or four vine-producing purple varieties found throughout most of the Mountain Northwest, all share very close similarities with *Clematis columbiana*, which grows on wooded, bushy mountain slopes. Of the cream-colored varieties, *Clematis ligusticifolia* serves as a good reference. This variety grows in riparian habitats and other moist areas, from deserts to montaine forests throughout North America. *C. columbiana* is a creeping vine that produces light-lavender to purple-blue flowers from the ends of its leafless flower stems. Flowers are axillary; with each flower stem growing from the crotch between branches and the main plant stem. **The flowers have four, lanceolate petals with yellow stamens in the center. Leaves are opposite and divided into three distinct, lance-shaped sections that appear indented on their margins.** Stems are strong and somewhat woody. Where Clematis grows in disorganized tangles among the mountain shrubs (which is usually the case with *C. columbiana*) it often goes unnoticed until its showy, purple flowers present themselves. The flowers are pleasingly long-lived, often blooming from

84

Clematis

May through July. The *Clematis ligusticifolia* variety is commonly seen as thick mats that can cover tree trunks and brush along riverbanks and other riparian areas. **Perhaps the most distinguishing characteristic of this variety is the profusion of silvery-white plumes of seed-carrying fluff that the plant produces after flowering.** Although *C. columbiana* also produces fluffy plumes, they are generally not as dramatic in presentation. *C. ligusticifolia* produces cream-colored flowers that have five petals and stamens of the same color. The plant often displays only the stamens... no petals at all. Leaves are similar to the purple varieties, but are divided into 5-7 parts, as opposed to just 3.

HABITAT
Clematis columbiana (purple flowers) grows on brush covered, wooded mountain slopes above 3000', but seldom higher than 8500'. *Clematis ligusticifolia* is very common at elevations below 3500', in riparian areas and gullies where it can climb all over neighboring plants and trees.

ACTIONS
Many references list this species as poisonous, even though it was widely used by Native Americans as a remedy for sore throats and colds. It is a diaphoretic, diuretic, and offers a unique vasoconstrictory/dilating action that makes it specifically useful in the treatment of migraine headaches.

PROPAGATION & GROWTH CHARACTERISTICS
Clematis is a perennial that produces viable seeds that generally need cold, moist stratification in order to germinate. Most varieties prefer shade and must have something to climb on. *Clematis columbiana* is sometimes available through nurseries, particularly those that specialize in native plants. Clematis is a beautiful addition to a shady trellis. It is slow to start from seed and does not transplant well from wild habitats.

Clematis

GATHERING SEASON AND GENERAL GUIDELINES
Gather the plant late in its bloom period or shortly thereafter. Don't wait too long, as the leaves die-back very quickly after the plant goes to seed. Pluck leaves or gather stems and all after the plant has seeded. Be careful not to damage neighboring plants when extricating the strong, entangled vines from brush.

PARTS USED
Leaves, stems, and flowers.

CARE AFTER GATHERING
This herb can be used in the field for acute-onset migraines by simply chewing the leaves. The leaves have a very peppery taste that tends to "bite the tongue". Generally speaking, the stronger the "bite", the more potent the plant's active constituents. I usually taste a small piece of the leaf to determine herb strength before I pick it. **However, please note that this plant is considered by many as toxic, and a sudden rush of light-headedness often results from the plant's vascular actions.** Clematis can be dried for short-term storage, but is best if used fresh. TINCTURE FRESH LEAVES and STEMS AT A 1:5 Ratio; 50% alcohol.

COMMON COMPANION HERBS
Pipsissewa, Oregon Grape, Strawberry, and *Uva-ursi* are but a few.

PLANT/ANIMAL INTERDEPENDENCE
The strong, often mat-forming stems of Clematis provide habitat and nesting materials for birds and other small animals. The long-lasting flowers are effective and important pollinator-attractors.

IMPACT CONSIDERATIONS
This is a strong herb if gathered at its medicinal prime. It has a very short shelf life if not tinctured immediately, and

Clematis

therefore should be tinctured in the field. It is generally not used very often, and probably shouldn't be in view of its controversial reputation as a toxic plant... so gather conservatively if you need some. When gathering on steep slopes wear adequate footwear and carry a walking stick to avoid slipping and unnecessary impact. If you are venturing into thick brush, be aware of the possible presence of small animals and their dwellings.

PHOTO REFERENCES
The Audubon Society Field Guide to North American Wildflowers, Richard Spellenberg
Forest Wildflowers, Dr. Dee Strickler
Edible and Medicinal Plants of the Rocky Mountains and Surrounding Territories, Terry Willard, Ph.D.

TECHNICAL REFERENCES
Medicinal Plants of the Mountain West, Michael Moore
Quick Reference - Medicinal Plants of the Northern Rockies, Mary Wulff-Tilford
Edible and Medicinal Plants of the Rocky Mountains and Neighbouring Territories, Terry Willard Ph.D. (also has a good photo)

STAND LOCATIONS

Date of Discovery	Location and Description of Stand	Site Record #

Coptis

Coptis spp.   Ranuculaceae

Impact Level: 3

OTHER NAMES
Gold Thread, Western Gold Thread, Yellowthread, Canker Root.

DESCRIPTION
Coptis is a low growing, evergreen perennial that is frequently found as the predominant ground cover in dense coniferous forests of the Mountain Northwest. **Leaves consist of three, wire-like petioles, each bearing a shiny leaflet that looks like a cross between a strawberry leaf and a small oak leaf.** Leaflets are ovate, 3-lobed, sharply toothed, and glossy on their upper surface. Each individual leaflet is generally under 1½" in width. **The entire plant is rarely more than 6" in height.**

The flowers of Coptis grow at the ends of **simple, leafless stems that extend away from the base of the plant.** The 1-3 whitish flowers have five to eight narrow sepals that are ¼"-½" long, and 5-7 narrower petals. When the petals fall off, the remaining green sepals create an odd appearance that could lead one to believe that the plant produces green, star-like flowers. These sepals remain on the plant to produce a multitude of hollow, dry, seed-bearing capsules that spread apart upon maturity.

The roots of Coptis are thin and often thread-like, with inner tissue that is a bright, goldenrod yellow. Roots are in the form of long, weak rhizomes, and have a bitter taste that is characteristic of all herbs which contain considerable amounts of the alkaloid *berberine.*

Coptis

HABITAT

Coptis occidentalis is common to shady, coniferous forests throughout Northern Idaho, the mountains of Eastern Washington, Montana, and British Columbia. It is particularly common in undisturbed stands of Cedar, Yew, and Grand Firs; where ample shade and a thick accumulation of forest debris is present. It is generally found at elevations above 2500', but seldom higher than 7000'.

Other varieties of Coptis can be found throughout the Eastern U.S and Eastern Canada, as well as more southern areas of the Rockies and the Pacific Northwest. All are very similar in appearance and are equally useful. Check with your local herbarium or a vascular plant reference that is specific to your region for the species native to your bioregion.

ACTIONS

This herb is of particular importance to the EcoHerbalist because it is an excellent alternative to Goldenseal... an herb that has been all but wiped out in its natural habitat.

The primary active ingredients in Coptis are *berberine* and *coptine.* Berberine is a bitter alkaloid that is very effective as a bitter digestive stimulant and possesses strong antibacterial qualities.

Coptis can be used like Goldenseal as a cholagogue, laxative, astringent, anti-inflammatory, uterotonic, and hemostatic.

PROPAGATION & GROWTH CHARACTERISTICS

Coptis is a perennial shade plant that requires plenty of rich, undisturbed organic matter in order to survive. It does not transplant well, probably because of the delicate nature of the stringy, rather small rhizomes. Coptis seeds are small and hard to collect. To do so, the gatherer must anticipate the period immediately prior to the opening of the mature fruits, or the seeds are lost. Immature seeds are generally not viable.

Coptis

Coptis is a very hardy plant, and can still be found in good condition beneath a blanket of snow.

GATHERING SEASON AND GENERAL GUIDELINES
Gather Coptis during dry weather and after it has bloomed and gone to seed. The rhizomes are generally found within the mat of forest debris, not in the soil beneath, which makes them very vulnerable to human feet. Gather from the edges of stands that are accessible without leaving a well-established foot trail.

Grasp the plant at its base and *gently* pull the plant up, until no more than three inches of the rhizome is exposed... then clip it off with sharp pruning shears. In areas where the forest compost is especially thick and spongy, a gentle pull will often meet little resistance, and the roots will come up like lengths of thread that are being pulled through lawn clippings. This makes for easy gathering, but it also means that you are probably in an area where serious impact will likely result from your being there. Avoid the "easy harvest". *This plant does not tolerate human impact.*

PARTS USED
Although most herbalists prefer to use only the root, we use the upper parts as well to eliminate waste.

CARE AFTER GATHERING
The fresh dried root can be chewed or made into a mouthwash (infusion) for treating mouth ulcerations, canker sores, etc. Although dried herb can be used, the fresh plant makes the best tincture. Whenever possible, make your tincture in the field. This eliminates all guess work in terms of how much to harvest, and yields medicine of optimum quality.
TINCTURE FRESH ROOT, STEM, AND LEAVES: 1:2 Ratio; 50% alcohol. DRIED WHOLE PLANT: 1:5 Ratio; 50% alcohol.

Coptis

COMMON COMPANION HERBS
Wild Ginger, False Solomon's Seal, Pipsissewa, Pyrola.

PLANT/ANIMAL INTERDEPENDENCE
Like Wild Ginger, Coptis is a plant which is well adapted to fully shaded conditions that are generally prohibitive of plant growth. Where Coptis grows in such dark, forested areas, it is often the predominant plant of the forest floor. The rhizomatous nature of this plant's root system provides a means for soil aeration and water infiltration. The plant breaks up the continuity of an otherwise impervious mat of forest debris, allowing the entry of insects and microorganisms that are critical to the production of compost and the release of plant nutrients. This paves the way for companion plants that could not otherwise adapt. In turn, many of these other plants serve the needs of the pollinators and larger animals that also play important roles within the biocommunity.

These delicate and complex biocommunities rely heavily upon balances that are maintained through an uninterrupted interdependency between all involved organisms... if one element is removed, the collective whole will fail. In areas where plants like Coptis have been denuded, one often finds a blank, or at best... a sparsely vegetated forest floor.

IMPACT CONSIDERATIONS
Coptis is a common plant, but its habitat is becoming thousands of acres more rare every year. It is a resident of pristine forests that are quickly disappearing. It is also a plant that follows in the footsteps of one of the most exploited herbs in history... Goldenseal.

I am hoping that this book has helped to instill a personal desire to maintain an attitude of proactivity; one that allows the individual to see beyond his or her personal needs and into the natural realms of yesterday and tomorrow. Coptis and other valuable "alternative herbs" require such an attitude if they are to survive future consumerism. Coptis is

Coptis

an herb that offers itself to us despite the shadow of greed and abuse humanity has cast upon its cousin, Goldenseal.   It is no less vulnerable, and every bit as valuable.   It offers us another chance to define what the word "value" really means, and to take a gift of healing to the heart, instead of to the bank.

Spend some time with Coptis before you harvest it. Learn and understand something about its special uniqueness... then gather with care.   Always be conscious of your impact and use your insight and imagination to reduce the effects subsequent to your visit.   Wear soft-soled shoes, or none at all, and walk deliberately.   Watch your footsteps... make sure that the forest carpet springs back quickly, leaving no lasting impressions.   Watch the stand over a period of *at least two years* following your harvest, and keep good notes of your observations.

Please, gather only what *you* need.   If a friend needs some, get that friend *involved; connected.*   Let's not repeat history.

PHOTO REFERENCES

Peterson Field Guides, Eastern/Central Medicinal Plants, Foster & Duke (also contains technical information)

Magic and Medicine of Plants, Reader's Digest Books

TECHNICAL REFERENCES

Medicinal Plants of the Pacific West, Michael Moore

Out of the Earth, Simon Y. Mills (refered to under *Goldenseal*)

Indian Herbalogy of North America, Alma R. Hutchens

Quick Reference - Medicinal Plants of the Northern Rockies, Mary Wulff-Tilford

Coptis

STAND LOCATIONS

Date of Discovery	Location and Description of Stand	Site Record #

Field Notes

Cow Parsnip

Heracleum lanatum   Umbelliferae

IMPACT LEVEL: 2

OTHER NAMES
Cow Cabbage, American Masterwort, Wild Parsnip, Wooly Parsnip, Wild Celery, Indian Celery.

DESCRIPTION
Like most members of the Carrot/Parsley family, Cow Parsnip has tiny, 5-petalled, white flowers arranged in umbrella-shaped clusters (umbels). Mature plants produce several of these umbels, but the one growing from the center stalk is generally the largest. After blooming, the umbels produce large (up to ¼") seeds that are flat on one side, and slightly rounded on the other, each with distinct ridges that alternate with four black lines. Leaves are very large, often growing to 10" or more, and are divided into three parts... much like a large maple leaf. Leaf margins are serrated.

Stems are stout and hollow, somewhat hairy, and grooved along their length.

Roots are large, tapered, light brown in color, and usually have a pungent, carrot-like odor. Cow Parsnip is one of the largest members of the Umbelliferae family, often reaching a height of over seven feet. Although many people shy away from Cow Parsnip because of its relationship to Water Hemlock, it shares similarity with this poisonous cousin only in its flower and habitat. Cow Parsnip has leaves that are not at all carrot-like, which makes it very easy to distinguish from Water Hemlock.

Cow Parsnip

Heracleum species

HABITAT
   Cow Parsnip likes wet, boggy soil and is often found growing along streams, springs and in wet meadows. It is seldom found more than a few feet from a constant source of water. It requires partial shade, and is widespread throughout North America from sea level to about 9000'.

ACTIONS
   Although not frequently used, Cow Parsnip has a long history as an effective remedy for the digestive and nervous systems. The seeds are analgesic to the teeth and gums, with application and effects that are similar to clove oil.

Cow Parsnip

PROPAGATION & GROWTH CHARACTERISTICS
A native perennial that reproduces by seed, Cow Parsnip is effectively distributed by run-off and through animal consumption. It can be propagated from seed if stratified and kept very moist throughout germination. Plants grow rapidly, producing a large taproot that requires rich, deep soil.

GATHERING SEASON AND GENERAL GUIDELINES
Collect the seeds during late summer, after they are ripe and display their dark stripes. Roots should be dug after the seeds have fallen from the plant, unless you are gathering the roots to eat, springtime is best (I have yet to hear of anyone that likes them). Like other Umbelliferaes, do not gather any part of this plant if it cannot be identified with absolute certainty. Although the plant is edible (not necessarily palatable) it has a reputation for causing a photosensitive contact-dermatitis in some individuals, so wear long sleeves and gloves when collecting seeds or roots. Do not gather Cow Parsnip if Water Hemlock is present.

PARTS USED
Roots or ripe seeds.

CARE AFTER GATHERING
According to herbalist Michael Moore, the roots should not be used fresh. Split or cut the roots lengthwise once or twice and dry with plenty of ventilation. Seeds can be used fresh or dried. TINCTURE ROOTS OR SEEDS: 1:2 Ratio with 50% alcohol.

COMMON COMPANION HERBS
Angelica, Horsetail, False Solomon's Seal, Cleavers, Mint family, Wild Ginger, and *Pyrola* are a few.

PLANT/ANIMAL INTERDEPENDENCE
Cow Parsnip is foraged upon throughout its growth period by deer, elk, moose, and bears. As its name implies,

Cow Parsnip

cows like it too. Its high-growing umbels are important pollinator-attractors. The plants large, leafy growth is an important source of shelter for insects and small animals, and often provides a cool, midday bed for larger animals. Shade-loving companion plant's are often found growing at Cow Parsnip's feet. The plants juicy leaves and stems decompose readily after dying back, and contribute considerable amounts of organic matter to the soil. The large root plays a natural role in anti-erosion and soil aeration.

IMPACT CONSIDERATIONS

The impact that is subsequent to gathering this herb varies according to the nature of each particular micro-ecosystem. If the plant is collected from mucky bogs and jungle-like growth, the wildcrafter's level of impact is likely to be very high. In instances where the plant is gathered from roadsides or next to a well-established trail, impact can be kept to a minimum. The extensive range and abundance of this plant leaves little excuse for incursions into vulnerable areas. Look for a healthy stand that is easy to access. Inspect prospective stands for evidence of active foraging... nibbled leaves, animal tracks or droppings. If feeding animals have been present, move on to another stand to avoid unnecessary vicarious impact. Gather during dry periods (but not drought) and wear soft footwear to minimize soil compaction. Monitor the area closely, and keep accurate records of any changes in the stand over a period of years.

PHOTO REFERENCES

Weeds of the West, The Western Society Of Weed Science

Nature Bound Pocket Field Guide, Ron Dawson (also contains some technical data)

TECHNICAL REFERENCES

Discovering Wild Plants, Janice J. Schofield

Medicinal Plants of the Mountain West, Michael Moore

Cow Parsnip

Edible and Medicinal Plants of the Rocky Mountains and Neighbouring Territories, Terry Willard, Ph.D.

Quick Reference - Medicinal Plants of the Northern Rockies, Mary Wulff–Tilford

STAND LOCATIONS

Date of Discovery	Location and Description of Stand	Site Record #

Dandelion

Taraxacum officinale Compositae

IMPACT LEVEL: 1

OTHER NAMES
Chicoria, Lion's Tooth.

DESCRIPTION
Come on... do you *really* need me to describe this plant for you? Actually this plant is misidentified more than most self-respecting herbalists care to admit. The main thing to bear in mind when gathering Dandelion is that the plant **has no leaf stems.** All of the leaves, and **the leafless flower stems** grow directly from the rootstalk in a rosette fashion. If the plant you are preparing to collect has **any sort of branching characteristic, then it is not a Dandelion.** Of the plants confused with Dandelion, Spotted Cat's Ear (*Hypochaeris radicata*) is perhaps the most common. When young the plant looks very similar, except for the rough, hairy characteristic of its leaves. At maturity, Spotted Cat's Ear grows much more erect than Dandelion and has flowers along its stems. Another plant that is commonly mistaken for Dandelion is Prickly Lettuce (*Lactuca serriola*). Again, this plant grows erect in maturity and develops branches off of the main stem. Also, when Prickly Lettuce is young, it has sharp spines along the back of its leaf midrib, unlike Dandelion.

HABITAT
Dandelion grows just about everywhere; from below sea level to about timberline. It likes full sun, but will grow with less flower development in shade. It tolerates any soil, but prefers rich, well drained loam with neutral acidity.

99

Dandelion

The aerial parts of Dandelion grow directly off of its root crown. Note the absence of any branches or leaf stems.

Leaves are smooth on upper and lower surfaces, unlike Lactuca serriola (Prickly Lettuce).

Taraxacum officinale

ACTIONS

A very safe and effective diuretic, Dandelion contains enough minerals (especially potassium) and vitamins to replace what is lost through the diuresis it stimulates. It is also antirheumatic, cholagogue, tonic and laxative. It contains a diversity of active constituents in safe quantities... it is an herb that is useful under almost any circumstances. Not enough can be said of this common and abundant plant's gift of well-being.

Dandelion

PROPAGATION AND GROWTH CHARACTERISTICS

No secrets here... Dandelion is a free-seeding perennial that often grows as an annual in severe climates. The problem of cultivating this herb in the garden is not so much growing it, but controlling it. Although this plant is considered a *"noxious weed"* throughout North America, Dandelion seed is available through some commercial seed suppliers. Dandelion is a popular salad green in Europe, but has not really caught on in our country. Hybrid food strains of this plant have been developed for consumer use.

GATHERING SEASON AND GENERAL GUIDELINES

The best leaves are plucked while green and juicy, just as the plant is beginning to bud, but can be gathered at any time. Roots can be dug anytime, although you may consider the project when the soil is damp and soft, as the often long taproots are difficult to extricate from hard, dry soil. We like to dig the large second or third year roots in early spring, when the leaves are green and juicy. This way we can gather both the leaves and roots in one trip. A round-nosed ditch shovel is highly recommended for digging this herb, as the roots are often *very* stubborn. The broad spectrum of medicinal applications of this plant and its abundance make it the front-line herb in our medicine chest. Mary and I often employ Dandelion first, or use it to supplement any number of other herbs. In consideration of its apparent willingness to relieve impact pressure from its plant companions, we gather and use more Dandelion than any other herb. **Since this wonderful plant is so widely hated, always be aware of the possible introduction of herbicides.** Do not gather Dandelion anywhere near a roadside or from cultivated fields unless you are absolutely certain that the area has not been sprayed within *at least the past three years.* That's right, herbicide residues are sometimes present in the environment for three years after application... we do not gather from areas that have *any* history of weed control efforts.

Dandelion

PARTS USED
The whole plant.

CARE AFTER GATHERING
The leaves and the roots can be used fresh or dried. If you are using the leaves for tea, we recommend that you dry them first, as the fresh leaves tend to taste bitter. For tincturing, the fresh root is best. Dry leaves and/or roots whole, on a non-metallic screen or newspapers. Roots should be cleaned of excess soil, etc. before drying. **Do not** wash the greens prior to drying, or mold will likely result. FRESH ROOT TINCTURE: 1:2 ratio; 45% alcohol. DRIED ROOT TINCTURE: 1:5 Ratio; 45% alcohol.

COMMON COMPANION HERBS
Dandelion does not care who it lives with; the possibilities here are endless.

PLANT/ANIMAL INTERDEPENDENCE
Although it is generally considered a troublesome weed by non-herbalists, Dandelion has many redeeming qualities as a contributor to the environment. A European import, Dandelion has brought to its new home a wealth of mineral-rich composted matter and an abundant source of early season food and incentive for the pollinator community. The persistent taproots are effective in breaking up the hardest of hardpan soils, and often play critical roles in erosion control. Dandelion is an enjoyable food plant for a multitude of animals, and absorbs much of the burdens during insect infestations and drought. Dandelion was introduced into North America largely through human impact, but has subsequently repaired much of the real damage we have caused. I view this plant as sort of a "mind herb", because it offers to us many lessons in perseverance and unconditional self-sacrifice.

Dandelion

IMPACT CONSIDERATIONS

Dandelion is a "free spirit plant" that distributes its seeds upon the wind, by run-off, animal consumption, or any other means beyond imagination. Remember your status as a natural visitor when you gather Dandelion and be careful to avoid carrying seeds into an alien environment. If the plant is gathered after it has gone to seed, this is nearly impossible, so gather Dandelion early on. Leave seed distribution to the plant and its natural allies. Introduction of Dandelion into new ecosystems can lead to chemical disaster.

Remember that many state, federal, and local agencies as well as individuals have waged all-out chemical warfare against this herb... check for herbicides before you harvest.

PHOTO REFERENCES

Nature Bound Pocket Field Guide, Ron Dawson
The Audubon Society Field Guide to North American Wildflowers, Richard Spellenberg
Northwest Weeds, Ronald J. Taylor
Weeds of the West, Western Society of Weed Science

TECHNICAL REFERENCES

Wise Woman Herbal - Healing Wise, Susun S. Weed
The New Age Herbalist, Richard Mabey
Discovering Wild Plants, Janice J. Schofield
Medicinal Plants of the Mountain West, Michael Moore
The Herb Book, John Lust
Quick Reference - Medicinal Plants of the Northern Rockies, Mary Wulff-Tilford

Echinacea

Echinacea spp.   Compositae

IMPACT LEVEL 4

OTHER NAMES
Purple Coneflower, Black Samson, Rudbeckia, Missouri Snakeroot.

DESCRIPTION
This profile is for identification and propagation purposes only. I am strongly opposed to wildcrafting Echinacea, regardless of its apparent proliferation in some micro-ecosystems.

Echinacea is a naturally long-lived perennial that ranges from 6"-40" in height. The genus is characterized by its dark, distinctively cone-shaped flower center. Flowers have drooping petals that range in color from pale purple-pink to deep purple (depending upon species) and are 2" to about 5" in diameter. The shape of the flower places Echinacea as an obvious member of the Sunflower Family.

Leaves are lanceolate to nearly oval. The leaves of the *Echinacea purpurea* variety are toothed, whereas other varieties generally are not.

HABITAT
Echinacea's rapid decline in the wild is in no small part due to a loss of suitable habitat. A native to prairies, open meadows, and sunny woodland clearings, Echinacea used to grow in abundance from the Continental Divide eastward. Where it used to flourish in the Plains States, Central Corn Belt, and the South, it has been drastically impacted by the advent of large-scale commercial farming.

104

Echinacea

A few isolated stands have been introduced into areas west of the Continental Divide.

ACTIONS

Echinacea is an effective, time-proven immunostimulant that was widely used by the Native Americans. Today it remains as perhaps the most well-known and sought after medicinal herb in North America... perhaps the world. Recent scientific validation and an effective media-marketing campaign have made Echinacea an herbal sensation. It's not all hype... with the global focus on our increasingly depressed auto-immune system, Echinacea has brought new hope to the realm of conventional western medicine. I have heard of cases where Echinacea has been prescribed by western allopathic physicians. Although I have to take my hat off to the recognition of an herb as medicine among western doctors, I am disappointed in the narrow focus of attention that has been put on a single herb because of good marketing strategies. There are many other herbs that offer immunostimulating qualities that should be given equal attention... herbs that could relieve some of the consumer pressure bestowed upon Echinacea.

PROPAGATION & GROWTH CHARACTERISTICS

Echinacea is fast becoming the herb to grow in North America. Most species are easy to grow and require little care once they are established. Seeds require cold, damp stratification (90 days for *E.angustifolia* & *E.pallida*) and light to break their dormancy. This means that the seeds must be sown atop the soil, or covered with just a trace of soil in order to germinate.

Roots must be at least three years old to be of medicinal value.

The tedious task of starting Echinacea in the herb garden is well worth the effort. The plants are hardy to at least Zone 4 and are very drought-tolerant when mature. A well established stand of Echinacea will reseed itself, and

Echinacea

mature plants can bear roots of up to three pounds each.

Some nurseries sell young Echinacea plants as perennial landscape flowers. Check with your local suppliers for the varieties and cultural information suited to your area.

IMPACT CONSIDERATIONS

Due to loss of habitat and greedy, selfish, totally irrational wildcrafting, wild stands of Echinacea are quickly being wiped out. In the South, East, and Central portions of America, Echinacea is often erradicated by commercial wildcrafters as quickly as it is discovered. Bearing in mind that it takes three years to produce useable roots, the quality of commercially wildcrafted Echinacea is very questionable.

Please do not wildcraft this herb. The survival of this beautiful flower is dependent upon organic farming and a large measure of luck on part of the remaining wild plants. If you are lucky enough to find a wild stand, keep it a secret and protect it. If the stand is in the form of an entire field, it may sadly be the last wild field of Echinacea you ever get to see... unless people change.

I urge you to plant Echinacea in your garden and to support your local organic grower.

106

Elderberry

Sambucus spp.   Caprifoliaceae

IMPACT LEVEL: 2

OTHER NAMES
Elder, Red Elder, Blue Elder, Black Elder.

DESCRIPTION
Elderberry is a shrub or many-branched small tree that grows to 25', but generally remains smaller at high elevations or in severe climates.

There are several varieties of Elderberry. Most people differentiate them by the color of their berries. The blue and black varieties are commonly gathered for use in jams, pies and Elderberry wine. **The red varieties have a reputation for being somewhat toxic... especially their seeds, leaves, bark, and roots.**

The leaves of Elderberry are pinnately compound, growing in 2-4 opposite pairs of lance-shaped 1"-5" leaflets, **with a single leaflet growing from the tip of each compound leaf.** Leaflets generally have saw-toothed margins with sometimes hairy under-surfaces.

Flowers are white to cream-colored, 5-lobed, and each about ¼" wide; growing in dense, upright clusters that are about 4" across. The flowers are fragrantly sweet. The clusters later develop the berries, which are often so abundant that their weight causes the branches to droop.

Elderberry is often confused with Mountain Ash (*Sorbus spp.*), a shrub or small tree that bears very similar leaves and clusters of bright-red berries. The leaves of Mountain Ash tend to be more ovate than those of Elderberry, **and have a serrated edge that points toward the tip of the**

107

Elderberry

leaflet. The leaves of Mountain Ash also tend to be more uniform in shape and smaller than those of Elderberry, and are often alternate, instead of opposite. Elderberry leaves are often very large and curl backward, much like peach leaves. The identification characteristics of both Elderberry and Mountain Ash usually become obvious to the wildcrafter after positive identification is accomplished in the field.

Sambucus racemosa

Elderberry

HABITAT

Found in moist soils of mountain hillsides and along roadsides and stream banks. Elderberry is frequently present in old clearcuts and burned areas, where it can enjoy lots of sun exposure and potassium-rich soil. Six or so species are common throughout the Western United States, at elevations ranging from sea-level to nearly 10,000'.

ACTIONS

Diaphoretic, diuretic, and an effective laxative.

PROPAGATION & GROWTH CHARACTERISTICS

Elderberry is a deciduous shrub that likes ample moisture and at least partial sun exposure. It can be started from seed, but is generally slow in becoming established. Wild shrubs do not transplant well at any stage. Many fruit tree nurseries sell Elderberry trees that are fast and easy to establish in a sunny spot in your yard. In its natural habitat, Elderberry is largely distributed by the wide variety of animals that eat the berries.

GATHERING SEASON AND GENERAL GUIDELINES

Flower clusters should be gathered *conservatively* when the buds are just beginning to open; usually sometime between mid-May and July. Berries are ready when they are fully ripe in mid to late summer, but before they begin to dry up.

Gather only the flower clusters and berries that are **within easy reach**. This will minimize damage to the tree and surrounding habitat.

PARTS USED

The flowers and berries; sometimes the leaves. **Caution: The seeds, leaves, bark, and roots all contain hydrocyanic acid and the alkaloid *sambucine*. These elements are toxic and can cause acute emetic and laxative effects.** Berries should be consumed only when ripe, and should be used for food only after cooking and the removal of seeds.

Elderberry

Flowers are much more gentle to the user.

CARE AFTER GATHERING
Flowers can be used fresh in tea, or for food recipes. Fresh berries are cooked and strained for jams. Both the flowers and berries can be dried for future medicinal use, but shelf life is limited to six months or less. Dry on non-metallic screens, newspapers, or in paper bags with the tops left open. Avoid exposure to sunlight during and after the drying process.

COMMON COMPANION HERBS
St. John's Wort, Mullein, Stinging Nettle, Red Osier, False Solomon's Seal, Oregon Grape... to name just a few.

PLANT/ANIMAL INTERDEPENDENCE
Elderberry is a very important food plant for birds and a wide variety of mammals. It provides a popular nesting habitat for our winged companions, and is a very effective pollinator-attractor during its profuse bloom period... sometimes the presence of this plant can be detected just by the sound of bees humming! Where Elderberry grows at roadside and in burned areas it plays important roles in habitat regeneration and erosion control.

IMPACT CONSIDERATIONS
This is an abundant herb that should be gathered conservatively from several different stand locations. Be aware of the possible presence of small animal and bird dwellings in and around this plant's branches. Do not gather from stands where active animal foraging is evident; especially where bears have been feeding. These ravenous animals often strip Elderberry shrubs of every juicy berry they can reach, thus making our vicarious impact a possibility to consider.

Visual impact upon this plant is always indicative of over-harvest. Get to know several Elderberry stands and their interdependent organisms before you start gathering.

110

Elderberry

PHOTO REFERENCES
The Audubon Society Field Guide to North American Wildflowers, Richard Spellenberg
Discovering Wild Plants, Janice J. Schofield
Forest Wildflowers, Dr. Dee Strickler

TECHNICAL REFERENCES
Medicinal Plants of the Mountain West, Michael Moore
The New Age Herbalist, Richard Mabey
The Holistic Herbal, David Hoffmann
The Herb Book, John Lust
Quick Reference - Medicinal Plants of the Northern Rockies, Mary Wulff-Tilford

STAND LOCATIONS

Date of Discovery	Location and Description of Stand	Site Record #

False Solomon's Seal

Smilacina racemosa/stellata   Liliaceae

IMPACT LEVEL. 2

OTHER NAMES
Solomon's Plume, Wild Lily-of-the-Valley.

DESCRIPTION
A very pretty inhabitant of the forest floor, False Solomon Seal's rhizomes creep through moist forest compost and emerge along their way as dark green, 8"-32" leafy stalks.

Leaves are alternate, 2½"-8" long, broadly lanceolate and often shiny (*S. racemosa).* The leaves of *S. stellata* are similar but smaller, narrower, and more sharply pointed.

Flowers appear in **terminate clusters** and are tiny, white, and star-shaped.

The stem is strong and has a slight, zig-zag growth characteristic. **Berries are in the form of reddish balls, often appearing as yellow with dark red stripes or spots... like miniature cantaloupes**.

Both *Smilacina racemosa* and *S. stellata* are commonly seen growing side by side. Both species are sometimes confused with a similar-looking cousin, *Streptopus spp.* (Twisted Stalk). **Twisted Stalk can be easily distinguished from False Solomon's Seal by its flowers, which oddly hang from little twisted stalks** *along* **the plant's stems** (unlike False Solomon's Seal, which has terminal clusters). The stems of Twisted Stalk generally have a more defined zig-zag pattern about them, **with leaves that wrap** *completely* **around the stem of the plant;** unlike the leaves of False Solomon's Seal, which grow more directly off of the stem.

112

False Solomon's Seal

HABITAT
False Solomon's Seal likes soil that is rich in organic matter. It is a common plant in shady coniferous forests, from sea level to nearly 10,000', throughout the Western U.S.. This plant often presents itself as the "predominant forest carpet plant" here in Western Montana.

ACTIONS
An effective demulcent and expectorant for upper respiratory infections.

PROPAGATION & GROWTH CHARACTERISTICS
False Solomon's Seal is a perennial that grows from its laterally-creeping roots. The plant is very difficult to start from seed, with a double dormancy that requires two years (and two stratification periods) in order for seeds to germinate. They require mostly shaded areas with soil that retains moisture well. Rhizome cuttings can sometimes be established in a sterile, damp medium (such as peat moss), but the odds are against you.

GATHERING SEASON AND GENERAL GUIDELINES
This herb can be dug anytime, but you may want to wait until flowers are present to alleviate any identification doubts.
Take the upper plant and only 3" or less of the rhizome, which is rather small and easy to damage. To avoid breaking the stem off above ground level, grasp the rhizome just below the soil and cut it with sharp scissors... leaving plenty of the root for next year's growth.

PARTS USED
The whole plant. Although only the root is preferred and used by most herbalists, the upper plant parts are also useable and should not be wasted.

False Solomon's Seal

CARE AFTER GATHERING

Although it is best if used fresh in cough syrups, it can be dried and stored for up to six months for use in tea. Spread the plants loosely on paper or a non-metallic screen and dry in a well ventilated location that is away from sunlight. Stir the plants often while drying to help prevent mold.

COMMON COMPANION HERBS

Pipsissewa, Wild Ginger, Coptis.

PLANT/ANIMAL INTERDEPENDENCE

The rhizomatous nature of this plant makes it an effective soil aerator. The rhizomes also help to hold together mats of coniferous debris that acts as moisture-retaining mulch for the forest floor biocommunity. The often extensive root systems form a "subterranean highway" for insects, small rodents, and microorganisms that play integral roles in the maintenance of an ecosystem.

IMPACT CONSIDERATIONS

Although this herb is abundant and widespread, the impact caused during its harvest is often unproportionately high. Gather False Solomon's Seal during periods when the forest floor is dry and resilient, to avoid unnecessary soil compaction. Avoid soft, mossy, consistently moist areas and places where the plant is growing within a proliferation of other growth.

A good rule-of-thumb in identifying compactable soils is to carefully watch your footsteps... if *soft-soled shoes* or bare feet create indentations that are more than ¼" deep and don't rebound quickly, then you are compacting soil and should find a different stand. The best place to gather is from stands that allow unobstructed access over firm soil.

Be aware of the possibility of creating vicarious impact. This herb is very vulnerable to the trampling of uncaring humans and livestock. In many areas where False Solomon's Seal grows along a stream, growth of this herb (and others)

114

False Solomon's Seal

has been heavily impacted by thirsty cows and careless recreationists.

Gather gently, conservatively, and monitor the stand closely for at least two years. Keep comprehensive records of regrowth and watch for any indications of vicarious impact.

PHOTO REFERENCES

Edible and Medicinal Plants of the Rocky Mountains and Surrounding Territories, Terry Willard, Ph.D. (contains *excellent* photos of this plant and Twisted Stalk)

The Audubon Society Field Guide to North American Wildflowers, Richard Spellenberg

Forest Wildflowers, Dr. Dee Strickler

TECHNICAL REFERENCES

Medicinal Plants of the Pacific West, Michael Moore

Quick Reference – Medicinal Plants of the Northern Rockies, Mary Wulff-Tilford

STAND LOCATIONS

Date of Discovery	Location and Description of Stand	Site Record #

Fireweed

Epilobium angustifolium   Onagraceae

IMPACT LEVEL: 2

OTHER NAMES
Willow Herb, Willow Weed, Blooming Sally.

DESCRIPTION
Fireweed is well known for its spires of brilliant pink flowers that give colorful contrast to burns and other disturbed areas throughout most of North America.

The flowers of Fireweed *(E. angustifolium)* are brightly colored, four-petalled, **and grow in terminal, spire-shaped clusters atop the erect stems.**

Leaves are narrowly lanceolate, 4"-6" long, and share a resemblance with many species of Willow (although this plant is unrelated to the *Salix* clan). The leaves are pale on their undersides; darker on top, and grow alternately in what often appears as an upward spiral along the main stem. **The veins of the leaves have a peculiar characteristic of joining together in loops at the leaf margins.**

The fruits of the plant are 2"-3" long, very slender, and stand rigidly off of the stem. These skinny pods eventually split open to release airborne, seed-bearing puffs of fine white hairs.

Two species of Fireweed are common to the Mountain Northwest, the aforementioned and *E. Latifolia.* Both species are similar in appearance and are often found growing together. Both are identically useful.

116

Fireweed

Epilobium angustifolium

HABITAT

Fireweed is best know for its proliferation at the edges of clearcuts, burned areas, and roadsides, but can also be found in undisturbed meadows up to about 10,000'.

Fireweed

ACTIONS
Fireweed tea is a pleasant, mild laxative. It is useful in settling an upset stomach. A decoction of the aerial parts is said to be useful as an antispasmodic in the treatment of whooping cough and asthma.

The young leaves and shoots are delicious in salads or if used as a potherb.

PROPAGATION & GROWTH CHARACTERISTICS
Fireweed is a perennial that propagates itself from spreading rhizomes and airborn seeds. It is very successful in establishing itself along the predominantly downwind edges of burns and other forest clearings.

Seeds germinate easily after a period of cold, moist stratification, with a few of the less common varieties requiring light to break their dormancy. Root cuttings can be transplanted with success if kept constantly moist until they are established.

Fireweed is not picky, but will do best in deep, well-drained soil that is high in potassium (wood ash is a good source). It prefers full sun for at least fours hours each day.

GATHERING SEASON AND GENERAL GUIDELINES
For medicinal use, Fireweed should be gathered while it is blooming (generally June–Sept.). Cut the stalk above ground level, taking care not to disturb the roots. If you desire to use the root, take only a few inches of the rhizome and leave the rest for perennial regrowth.

For food use, gather the young shoots and leaves, before the plants bloom in early spring. Although the older plants remain edible, the leaves tend to become bitter and tough later in life (such is the case with many wildcrafters). If you still wish to eat the plant during its maturity, use the tender leaf tips and side shoots.

Consumption of too much Fireweed is likely to cause dramatic utilization of toilet tissue.

118

Fireweed

PARTS USED
The whole plant.

CARE AFTER GATHERING
Although this herb is best when used fresh, the roots can be dried for use in salves or in powder form. The above-ground parts should be chopped and used fresh in tea.

COMMON COMPANION HERBS
Mullein, Stinging Nettle, Burdock, Dock, Dandelion...

PLANT/ANIMAL INTERDEPENDENCE
Fireweed is one of Nature's *Earth Regenerators*... it is a plant that establishes itself in order to renew defoliated areas.
Fireweed's rhizomes help to loosen compacted soils. The juicy leaves and stems contribute rich compost to the soil after die-back in the fall. A dense stand of Fireweed provides habitat for birds and small mammals that are rebuilding their livelihood, and a source of concealment for the larger animals that browse upon the foliage.
It is often the first substantial source of food and cover to appear in burned areas, providing many elements critical to the rebirth of a micro-ecosystem.

IMPACT CONSIDERATIONS
For the purpose of effective habitat regeneration, please do not gather Fireweed from areas that have been recently damaged by fire or other heavy impact. Leave such stands to complete their job, and find another stand in a well-established habitat.
Gather from the periphery of large stands, taking care not to disturb the habitat that the stand maintains. Better yet, find isolated plants that are growing away from the main stand and gather from those. Any visual impact upon a stand is indicative of over-harvest.
When gathering within clearcuts, burned areas, or other clearings that are a result of human impact, always be aware of

119

Fireweed

the potential for erosion and other forms of vicarious impact. Many times we will find this herb within areas that have already been thrown out of natural balance. The EcoHerbalist should carefully, and lovingly consider the possible effects of consumption from such areas.

PHOTO REFERENCES

Nature Bound Pocket Field Guide, Ron Dawson
Northwest Weeds, Ronald J. Taylor
Weeds of the West, The Western Society of Weed Science
Forest Wildflowers, Dr. Dee Strickler
The Audubon Society Field Guide to North American Wildflowers, Richard Spellenberg

TECHNICAL REFERENCES

Medicinal Plants of the Pacific West, Michael Moore
Discovering Wild Plants, Janice J. Schofield
Edible and Medicinal Plants of the Rocky Mountains and Neighbouring Territories, Terry Willard, Ph.D. (also has good photos)
Quick Reference - Medicinal Plants of the Northern Rockies, Mary Wulff-Tilford

STAND LOCATIONS

Date of Discovery	Location and Description of Stand	Site Record #

Goldenrod

Solidago spp. Compositae

IMPACT LEVEL: 1

OTHER NAMES
Western Goldenrod, Mountain Goldenrod, Sticky Goldenrod, Late Goldenrod, Canada Goldenrod, Missouri Goldenrod, Common Goldenrod, Blue Mountain Tea, Boheatea, Wound Weed.

DESCRIPTION
Goldenrods are "weedy" perennials that can grow as high as 5' in lower altitude, riparian habitats. Dryland species, particularly those at the higher elevations, may grow to 30", but are usually much shorter. Leaves are generally lance-shaped, alternate, simple, and may have toothed or untoothed margins.

Stems are generally strong, rigid, and erect.

Goldenrod is most commonly recognized by its **bushy, bright, *goldenrod-yellow* terminal clusters.** These clusters consist of dozens (often hundreds) of tiny florets which often have a sweet, honey-like odor.

HABITAT
The habitat in which Goldenrods choose to live varies according to species, although all of them require full sun. *S. occidentalis* (Western Goldenrod), *S. canadensis* (Canada Goldenrod), and *S. gigantea* (Late Goldenrod) all prefer moist, riparian habitats of valley floors and canyons; generally below 3500' in elevation.

Other Goldenrods, such as *S. missouriensis* (Missouri Goldenrod), *S. multiradiata* (Mountain Goldenrod), and *S.*

Goldenrod

spathulata (Sticky Goldenrod) are found in dry, open meadows and on south-facing slopes as high as 9000'.

Solidago represents a large, widely distributed genus. Several species are common thoughout North America.

Solidago species

Goldenrod

ACTIONS

Astringent, diuretic, carminative, diaphoretic, tonic. Used topically, dried Goldenrod in powder form is good for stopping the bleeding of minor cuts and scratches (ie., wherever a styptic pencil is indicated). Goldenrod tea is said to relieve hayfever symptoms if used prior to onset, **but should not be used by those who have already identified their allergy to the herb itself.** According to herbalist David Hoffman, "Goldenrod is perhaps the first plant to think of for upper respiratory catarrh, whether acute or chronic. It may be used in combination with other herbs in treatment of influenza." Goldenrod is also said to be useful in the treatment of urinary tract infections, kidney stones, and arthritis.

PROPAGATION & GROWTH CHARACTERISTICS

Most Goldenrods are rhizomatous perennials that reproduces from its rhizomes or from seed. Although many varieties will grow in the poorest of soils, most varieties prefer deep, rich loam.

This plant is considered a "troublesome weed" by many, but it is not highly competitive with other plants and is seldom found as the predominant plant of its habitat. Instead, it is usually found growing in small patches; often "dotting" a field or adding sporadic bursts of color to a streambank.

It is very easy to grow in the garden. Goldenrod seed is available through retailers... look for seed companies or nurseries that offer a wildflower selection.

GATHERING SEASON AND GENERAL GUIDELINES

Gather this plant during its bloom (Aug.-Sept.). Clip the top 6"-12" of the plant with a sharp pair of shears, leaving plenty of other plants for reseeding and pollinator activity.

PARTS USED

Goldenrod

All above-ground parts.

CARE AFTER GATHERING
Dry this herb prior to using it for use as a styptic powder or as an ingredient in teas. This plant dries well if hung in loose bunches (no more than 1" wide at their bases) that have been covered with a single sheet of newspaper or a paper bag. The paper will keep the dust off and sunlight out without too much restriction of air circulation.

The dried herb can then be coarsely crushed for use in tea, or ground fine and used as a styptic powder.

To make an oil infusion, put the finely chopped, *freshly wilted* herb in a glass jar and cover with olive oil. Use enough oil to cover the herb *completely...* if any air remains in contact with the herb, spoilage will likely occur. Cover the jar with a tight-fitting lid and allow it to sit for at least a month before straining. The oil is then useful for topical salves, ointments, or by itself.

COMMON COMPANION PLANTS
It is interesting to note that the *S. canadensis* variety is usually found growing with plant species that are of the same size. Aside from this bit of trivia, the neighborhood possibilities are nearly limitless.

PLANT/ANIMAL INTERDEPENDENCE
Goldenrod's claim-to-fame in Nature is its ability to attract pollinators from miles around. Its sweet flowers also attract ants and other insects, and sometimes the foraging deer.

IMPACT CONSIDERATIONS
Given the usefulness and abundance of this plant, one can only assume that its relatively infrequent medicinal application is due to the marketplace sensationalism of other herbs. While natural populations of "trendy herbs" (such as Osha' and Eyebright) are being seriously compromised by

Goldenrod

consumer demands that may not even specifically match their medicinal offerings, Goldenrod (notably a weed) stands undisturbed. Goldenrod is here... it's abundant... it's prolific... *it's in your backyard, let's use it!*

PHOTO REFERENCES
>*The Audubon Society Field Guide to North American Wildflowers,* Richard Spellenberg
>*Weeds of the West,* Western Society of Weed Science
>*The New Age Herbalist,* Richard Mabey (also has some technical information)
>*Peterson Field Guides – Eastern/Central Medicinal Plants,* Foster & Duke (also some technical information)

TECHNICAL REFERENCES
>*Discovering Wild Plants,* Janice J. Schofield (also has a good photo)
>*The Holistic Herbal,* David Hoffmann
>*The Herb Book,* John Lust
>*An Elder's Herbal,* David Hoffmann

STAND LOCATIONS

Date of Discovery	Location and Description of Stand	Site Record #

Horehound

Marrubium vulgare   Lamiaceae

IMPACT LEVEL: 1

OTHER NAMES
White Horehound, Marrubio.

DESCRIPTION
Unlike other members of the Mint Family, **Horehound has little or no odor.** Otherwise, it is characteristically another mint... square stems, opposite leaves, and flowers at leaf axils.

Stems and leaves of Horehound are distinctively wooly. Leaves are ovate, ½"-1½", wrinkled, and coarsely toothed.

Flowers are tiny, white, and present themselves in clusters that later develop into bunches of small, spiny burrs.

The plant often becomes densely branched when mature, and can grow up to 3' in height... but is usually found in low-growing clumps.

HABITAT
Horehound is a Eurasian import that has found its way into dry disturbed areas throughout the United States. It is a common inhabitant of vacant lots and roadsides, at all subalpine elevations.

ACTIONS
A time-proven expectorant and bitter tonic. Horehound is still used in many commercial brands of cough drops.

Horehound

PROPAGATION & GROWTH CHARACTERISTICS
Horehound is a deep rooted perennial that isn't picky about soil quality. It likes hard, dry gravel or clay that is low in organic matter. Although the plant will flourish in deep, rich soils, the best Horehound is found in the former.

It is an easy plant to establish from seed or transplants, and is an excellent addition to the herb garden.

GATHERING SEASON AND GENERAL GUIDELINES
Pick the good basal leaves after the plant has bloomed and seeds have started to form, or clip whole stems with sharp shears, leaving plenty of flowers for reseeding.

PARTS USED
Primarily the leaves, but all aerial parts are useful.

CARE AFTER GATHERING
Use fresh for a gross tasting but effective tea or cough syrup. FRESH PLANT TINCTURE: 1:5 Ratio (herb:alc); 50% alcohol (100 proof).

COMMON COMPANION HERBS
Pineapple Weed, Mullein, Hound's Tongue, Dandelion, or just about any other weedy herb that has a masochistic tendency.

PLANT/ANIMAL INTERDEPENDENCE
Horehound often grows as an Earth Regenerator, and usually remains within its chosen biocommunities forever, once it is established. This plant provides a dependable source of cover for small animals and insects in areas where other cover may be scarce... such as the edges of dirt roads.

Horehound is an effective pollinator-attractor, and contributes at least small amounts of organic matter to the depleted soils it resides in. Its deep root system is effective in preventing erosion.

Horehound

IMPACT CONSIDERATIONS

Like all imported plants, it is not a good idea to introduce Horehound into an area where it does not already exist... beware of hitch hiking seeds.

Assess the quality of insect and small animal cover before gathering, and define the plant's roles in land maintenance as well. Soil compaction is generally not a concern when gathering this herb, but this should not be taken for granted.

Always leave plenty for our companion organisms to enjoy.

PHOTO REFERENCES

Weeds of the West, Western Society of Weed Science

The New Age Herbalist, Richard Mabey (also contains good technical info).

Peterson Field Guide, Eastern/Central Medicinal Plants, Foster & Duke

TECHNICAL INFORMATION

Medicinal Plants of the Mountain West, Michael Moore

The Holistic Herbal, David Hoffman

Quick Reference - Medicinal Plants of the Northern Rockies, Mary Wulff-Tilford

Horehound

STAND LOCATIONS

Date of Discovery	Location and Description of Stand	Site Record #

Field Notes

Horsetail

Equisetum arvense   Equisetaceae

IMPACT LEVEL 2

OTHER NAMES
Scouring Rush, Jointed Grass, Puzzle Grass, Pewterwort.

DESCRIPTION
There are several species of Horsetail, but all have a distinctively **jointed stem that looks like a cross between an asparagus shoot and a stalk of bamboo.**

All species are useful and identical in application, however, *Equisetum arvense* is the most popular variety among herbalists. The more delicate structure of *E. arvense* make it more water or alcohol soluble than the other, tougher varieties. For this reason, I will focus this herb profile on the *E. arvense* species of Horsetail.

Horsetail always grows in or very near to water. If water is not visible around the plant, then water is certainly available within a few feet of the soil surface. The plant produces two separate growths from its creeping rhizomes. The first is a branchless, tan-colored stalk that is void of any chlorophyll. This odd-looking shoot is short-lived and is reproductively fertile, producing spores from its conical tip. It appears in early spring, a week or more before the emergence of the plant's green, sterile stalk, and then dies back a short time thereafter.

The sterile, green stems are the ones that are of medicinal value.

The hollow stems of these sterile counterparts have

130

Horsetail

long, rounded grooves and can grow to 3', but are commonly within one foot.
Stems produce bushy whorls of green, horsehair-like branches from below the scale-like leaves that are at each stem joint. This gives the plant the appearance of a green bottle brush. Early in growth these little branches point upward, later on they will droop downward.

HABITAT
Horsetail frequents moist meadows and wooded areas, streambanks and lakeshores from sea level to about 10,000'. Members of the *Equisetum species* are often seen growing directly out of the water in mountain lakes. Most varieties prefer at least partial shade and deep, rich soil.

ACTIONS
Diuretic, coagulant, and hemostatic. The high silica content of this herb makes it effective in strengthening bones and connective tissue. It is an excellent cleanser for the skin and hair, and is even good for scouring dishes (hence the common name,"Scouring Rush"). The abrasive nature of this herb's constituents can cause urinary tract and kidney irritations in long term use, so moderation is advised.

PROPAGATION & GROWTH CHARACTERISTICS
Horsetail usually grows as a perennial, with some varieties (such as *E. hyemale*) growing pretty much as evergreens. In areas where climatic conditions are severe or impact levels are consistently high, Horsetail may appear as an annual.
Although possible, attempts at cultivation of Horsetail are generally futile. Rhizomes generally do not transplant well, and the nearly microscopic spores must be collected at their moment of optimum fertility for immediate distribution. Although the germination rates of the spores are generally low, I would opt for this method of propagation. Distribute the spores beneath a dripping spigot or in a moist drainage area.

Horsetail

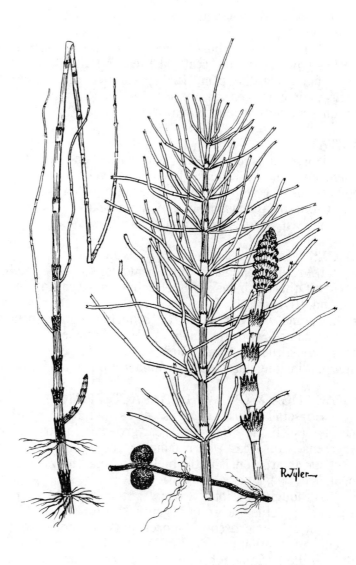

Equisetum arvense

Horsetail

GATHERING SEASON AND GENERAL GUIDELINES

Gather the sterile (green) stems while their little branches are still pointing upward (generally mid-spring). Older plants are still useful, but the silica constituents tend to crystallize with age, making the plant less soluble. Gather from the periphery of dense, healthy stands, taking care not to compact any more soil than is absolutely necessary to access the plants. Clip the stems with sharp pruning clippers, an inch or more above ground level.

According to herbalist Michael Moore, Horsetail should not be gathered from areas that are heavily fertilized; or from areas of high irrigation run-off, as Horsetail readily stores nitrates and selenium. For the same reason it is wise to be wary of areas that are grazed by livestock... such areas are often subject to the use of herbicides.

PARTS USED

The whole upper plant.

CARE AFTER GATHERING

Like all herbs that are gathered from a moist environment, Horsetail needs ample air circulation and dry conditions to prevent it from developing mold. Small bunches (1" or less) can be tied and hung in an airy, lightless location... or spread the plants on a non-metallic surface and stir them frequently.

This herb should be dried prior to use to allow for solubility. Use in small frequent doses (1 tsp. in a cup of hot water) if used in teas, bearing in mind that large amounts over a short timespan can cause urinary tract irritations. The dried herb can be tinctured as well. TINCTURE DRIED HERB: 1:5 Ratio; 50% alcohol.

COMMON COMPANION HERBS

Cow Parsnip, Angelica, Cleavers, Wild Ginger, False Solomon's Seal, Stinging Nettle, Mint Family...

Horsetail

PLANT/ANIMAL INTERDEPENDENCE

The rhizomatous nature of this plant benefits the structure of the wet soil it lives in. This is particularly true where Horsetail lives at the edge of moving water, where the plant's roots help maintain habitat for its companions by preventing erosion.

A stand of Horsetail is a common shelter for birds, reptiles, and amphibians. It is fascinating to realize that these creatures are descendants of those that also used Horsetail... *300 million years ago!* Horsetail is one of the oldest inhabitants of our planet, and have changed very little since before they were foraged upon by dinosaurs. Today they are foraged upon by deer and moose, and the dinosaurs that we now know as birds.

It would be arrogant and inexcusably ignorant to assume that such an Elder of the Earth does not serve critical roles within an ecosystem. This is a plant that has alot to teach us.

IMPACT CONSIDERATIONS

The impact that we bestow upon Horsetail and its often delicate habitat is relative to the depth of our understanding and respect. The soil that this herb grows in is often vulnerable to the effects of human feet. Whenever possible, gather from the margins of the driest stands you can find, and avoid those that are among a profusion of other plant growth. Learn and be aware of the rich diversity of life within riparian habitats, and stay alert for subtle movement and sounds during your visits.

Horsetail is an ancient plant-being that can teach us Earthly things beyond our imaginations... if we open our hearts and minds and take the time to learn. I find it both frightening and sad to think that after 300 million years Horsetail is now vulnerable to selfish, uncaring humans.

Horsetail

PHOTO REFERENCES
Discovering Wild Plants, Janice J. Schofield (good technical info too)
Peterson Field Guides, Eastern/Central Medicinal Plants, Foster & Duke
Nature Bound Pocket Field Guide, Ron Dawson

TECHINCAL REFERENCES
Wise Woman Ways - Menopausal Years, Susun S. Weed
The Male Herbal, James Green
Medicinal Plants of the Mountain West, Michael Moore
The Holistic Herbal, David Hoffmann
The Herb Book, John Lust
Quick Reference - Medicinal Plants of the Northern Rockies, Mary Wulff-Tilford

STAND LOCATIONS

Date of Discovery	Location and Description of Stand	Site Record #

Hound's Tongue

Cynoglossum officinale   Boraginaceae

IMPACT LEVEL 1

OTHER NAMES

Dog Burr, Dog's-tongue, Gypsy Flower, Sheep-lice, Woolmat.

DESCRIPTION

Hound's Tongue is a member of the Borage Family, with an appearance that immediately brings its close relative, Comfrey, into mind.

The leaves of Hound's Tongue grow opposite of one another, are lance-shaped, rough and hairy in texture, 1"-3" wide and up to 12" long. The plant produces a basal rosette of leaves the first year that die back in the fall. The second year of growth produces a central, flowering stalk that may reach as high as four feet.

Flowers are reddish-purple and present themselves terminally, like a loosely arranged bouquet at the top of the mature plant.

The flowers develop into **flat, tongue-shaped burrs that have a remarkable ability to stick to** *anything,* **with adherence that brings to mind the characteristics of Velcro.** The seeds can remain on the dead stalk for quite some time, turning light-gray and allowing for easy late-season identification.

The root is long and tapered.

HABITAT

Hound's Tongue is a European import that has found its home in pastures, ditches, and at roadsides across North America. Although it has a reputation of being toxic to

Hound's Tongue

livestock, it is curiously common to areas that have been disturbed by free-ranging cattle (the cows appear to be just fine).

Hound's Tongue is not particular about its habitat, but prefers constantly disturbed areas where it can cling to the passerby. It is very common on the margins of trails and roadways, from sea level to about 9000'.

ACTIONS

Hound's Tongue is a good alternative to Comfrey. Like its relative, it contains *allantoin* and the alkaloid *heliosupine.* It is a very effective topical application for skin irritations, particularly insect bites, and is useful internally as a sore throat and cough remedy.

Like Comfrey, care and moderation is warranted in its use, as it contains a quantity of potentially carcinogenic alkaloids.

PROPAGATION & GROWTH CHARACTERISTICS

No secrets here! Hound's Tongue is a very successful weed in North America. It is easy to start from seed, and if introduced into the herb garden it will take over if allowed. It is a biennial that may grow as a perennial, depending upon its natural needs or stubborn desires.

The plant's seed distribution effectiveness becomes obvious once you have wrestled the burrs from your clothing or Fido's coat.

GATHERING SEASON AND GENERAL GUIDELINES

Gather this plant when it is just beginning to bloom, generally in late spring or early summer. Dig the roots with a narrow, sharp shovel (such as a ditch spade), taking care not to disturb any of its less durable plant companions.

If you end up gathering roots after the plant has gone to seed, carefully remove any hitchhiking burrs from your clothing, hair, dogs, etc. before moving on. This plant is hated by many non-herbalists, and is often the target of

Hound's Tongue

herbicidal warfare. Check with your local Extension Office or other authorities for "weed abatement" (ie., land poisoning) programs in your area before you begin gathering, and always bear in mind that introduction of this plant into new areas can lead to the introduction of chemicals as well.

Don't gather this herb within 100' of any roadway, as it tends to absorb lead compounds and accumulates impurities on its hairy surfaces.

PARTS USED
The whole flowering plant, including the root.

CARE AFTER GATHERING
The fresh herb can be used as an ingredient in cough syrup or in tea, but the latter is generally more pleasant to the palate if dried herb is used.

Dry the upper plant and the chopped root on paper or a non-metallic screen, away from sunlight and with plenty of air circulation. Be absolutely certain that no moisture remains in the herb when you store it in an airtight container (unless compost is your goal). The dried herb will remain in quality condition for about six months.

COMMON COMPANION HERBS
Mullein, Dandelion, Horehound, Bee Balm, Burdock, Dock, Pineapple Weed...

PLANT/ANIMAL INTERDEPENDENCE
The long taproot of this plant is of great benefit to high impact areas where erosion may present a problem. The sturdy, persistent roots can penetrate hardpan soils, allowing aeration and the introduction of less adaptable plant companions.

The flowers of Hound's Tongue are effective pollinator-attractors, and the leaves provide shelter and habitat for beneficial insects and small animals. Where Hound's Tongue is growing at roadside, the shelter it provides often represents an

Hound's Tongue

immediate source of refuge for small animals and insects.

IMPACT CONSIDERATIONS

Hound's Tongue is an abundant plant that seems to be very resilient to human impact, but it is also one that is subject to the intent of herbicidal maniacs. For this reason we must consider our potential to create long-reaching vicarious impacts when we gather it. Care must be taken not to carry the burrs of this plant away from stands that are already established. Contrary to what the chemical companies may say, there are no herbicides with a capability of targeting one or a few specific plants. And *none* of them work without leaving unnatural and often harmful residues. This applies to organically approved, biological herbicides as well... many of these will not only kill a wide spectrum of plant life, but beneficial insect and animal communities are affected as well. It is unrealistic to believe that the introduction of *any* foreign agent into an ecosystem will *not* produce an unintended impact. And it would be selfish for the EcoHerbalist to avoid reponsibility for the prevention of a vicarious impact.

Please leave the seed distribution of this plant to our animal allies, and whenever possible try to discourage the use of *any* herbicides in natural environments.

PHOTO REFERENCES

Weeds of the West, The Western Society of Weed Science

Peterson Field Guides, Eastern/Central Medicinal Plants, Foster & Duke (drawings)

TECHNICAL REFERENCES

Medicinal Plants of the Mountain West, Michael Moore

Indian Herbalogy of North America, Alma R. Hutchens

Quick Reference - Medicinal Plants of the Northern Rockies, Mary Wulff-Tilford

Hound's Tongue

STAND LOCATIONS

Date of Discovery	Location and Description of Stand	Site Record #

Juniper

Juniperis spp. Cupressaceae

IMPACT LEVEL: 2

OTHER NAMES
"Cedar", Creeping Juniper, Prickly Juniper, Creeping Savin, Common Juniper.

DESCRIPTION
There are several species of Juniper in North America... all are medicinally useful. Generally they are differentiated by their size and growth characteristics; the tall, tree varieties, and the low-growing shrub varieties. All share intrinsically similar characteristics.

In the Mountain Northwest, *Juniperis communis*, or Common Juniper is the most abundant species. It is a low-growing shrub variety that can be found throughout North America, and it has a reputation among herbalists as having slightly stronger medicinal qualities than the larger varieties. It is this variety that I refer to in the following paragraphs.

Juniper is an evergreen shrub, 6"-40" tall, and is often found growing in circular patches that can be more than 20' wide. The branches lie flat or tend to curve slightly skyward, and are covered with small (½" long or less), sharp needles that have a whitish stripe on their upper surfaces.

The male cones of the shrub are small and inconspicuous, growing from the leaf axils. **The female berries develop terminally, and are purplish-blue with a whitish, dusty looking outer surface (like concord grapes have) when mature.**

Juniper

The entire shrub has a pleasant, distinctively aromatic quality to it that makes it a popular potpourri ingredient. The bruised berries are particularly pungent, with an odor that immediately identifies them as the primary ingredient in gin. The berries are quite tasty in their raw form, and are frequently used as a food seasoning, especially in the preparation of wild game.

HABITAT

Common Juniper is found within all elevation zones throughout the Mountain Northwest, but tends to be most abundant within the range of 5000'-9500'. It is partial to dry, rocky forest clearings and hillsides.

ACTIONS

The volatile oils in both the leaves and the stronger berries serve as an effective antiseptic, particularly in urinary tract disorders. The berries are also an effective bitter tonic, with carminative and diuretic qualities that compliment this function. **This herb can be irritating if over used, and should not be used in association with any kind of kidney disease or during pregnancy.**

Juniper berries are also said to relieve pain in the muscles and joints, and to ease the symptoms of arthritis and rheumatism when used topically.

PROPAGATION & GROWTH CHARACTERISTICS

Juniper is a drought-tolerant evergreen that is hardy down to at least -50°. It tolerates any soil, as long as there is ample structure (rocks, etc.) to hold its roots stable.

Juniper tends to be slow when started from seed and does not transplant well once it is established. Young shrubs can be purchased through commercial nurseries for introduction into the herb garden.

The berries of this plant require at least two years to reach maturity and ripen.

142

Juniper

GATHERING SEASON AND GENERAL GUIDELINES

Gather Juniper berries when they are dark blue and juicy. The leaves and branches can be gathered anytime. Be conservative. This plant serves as an important source of food and shelter for many of our animal companions, and it tends to regenerate slowly.

PARTS USED

The berries, leaves, and branches.

CARE AFTER GATHERING

Use the leaves and branches fresh, for teas or decoctions. The berries can be used fresh, either medicinally or for cooking; or they can be dried and stored for up to a year for future uses. For tincture, we use fresh berries, leaves, and the branches, although most herbalists are partial to just the berries.

TINCTURE FRESH BERRIES AND/OR LEAVES AND BRANCHES: 1:5 Ratio; 75% alcohol.

COMMON COMPANION HERBS

Pine, Arnica, Balsamroot, Oregon Grape, Penstemon, Yarrow...

PLANT/ANIMAL INTERDEPENDENCE

Juniper is an important source of forage for deer, elk, moose, bear, and rodents, but is especially relished by birds.

At our home in Western Montana, the gathering of Juniper berries from "the backyard bush" is largely regulated by the demands of the resident spruce grouse and the mobs of migrating grosbeaks and sparrows that pass through each year. For whatever is left, the squirrel that has made its home directly above the patch gets first choice, then a line is formed behind a collection of drooling deer, elk, and ground-dwelling rodents.

We are, of course, at the end of the line.

The low-growing, densely branched shrubs also provide

143

Juniper

cover and habitat for a wide variety of other organisms. Where Juniper lives on steep hillsides it helps to prevent erosion and to hold back nutrient-rich forest debris that might otherwise be washed away during heavy rain. In high alpine areas it is common to see Junipers growing directly out of rock fissures, with a collection of dependent flora growing from the alluvial accumulation at the bases of the shrubs.

IMPACT CONSIDERATIONS

The impact we cause through the harvest of Juniper strongly relates to our development of natural awareness and our familiarity with the micro-ecosystem we are working within. Juniper is an important food and shelter source for a wide variety of sometimes transient organisms. The potential for vicarious impact here is unlimited if we do not first become aquainted with the natural demands upon the plants we are intentionally impacting. As I mentioned in the previous section, the shrub near my house is frequented every year by migratory birds... this sort of knowledge is aquired over a period of years, and is critical in minimizing my harvest impact. But even my familiarity cannot foresee a drought, a fire, or next year's deer population increase.

Become as intimate as you can with a variety of Juniper stands. Then gather carefully and thoughtfully, attuned to any changes within each stand. *Keep records.*

Any visual impact whatsoever is indicative of over-harvest. Remember, your remedy or food seasoning may likely be the life source for several other beings.

PHOTO REFERENCES

Discovering Wild Plants, Janice J, Schofield (also has good techinical info.)

The Audubon Society Field Guide to North American Trees and Shrubs

Peterson Field Guides, Eastern/Central Medicinal Plants, Foster & Duke

The New Age Herbalist, Richard Mabey

Juniper

TECHNICAL REFERENCES
Medicinal Plants of the Mountain West, Michael Moore

The Holistic Herbal, David Hoffmann

Edible and Medicinal Plants of the Rocky Mountains and Neighbouring Territories, Terry Willard, Ph.D.

Magic and Medicine of Plants, Readers Digest Books

Quick Reference - Medicinal Plants of the Northern Rockies, Mary Wulff-Tilford

STAND LOCATIONS

Date of Discovery	Location and Description of Stand	Site Record #

Lomatium

Lomatium dissectum   Umbelliferae

IMPACT LEVEL: 3

OTHER NAMES
Biscuitroot, "Big Medicine", "Bear Medicine", Western Wild Parsley, Mountain Parsley, Fern-leaved Lomatium.

DESCRIPTION
Several varieties of the Lomatium species grow throughout the Mountain Northwest... eight varieties can be found in West-Central Montana alone. Of these varieties, only one has a reputation of being medicinally useful, *Lomatium dissectum*. The others are edible, hence the common name "Biscuit Root", but whether or not they possess the medicinal properties of *L. dissectum* has not been established.

Although all of the Lomatiums share intrinsic similarities in both appearance and habitat, *Lomatium dissectum* is easy to differentiate by its large size and showy leaves.

In structure and appearance, *Lomatium dissectum* is typically a member of the Carrot/Parsley Family, with umbel-shaped, terminal flower clusters, hollow stems, and leaves that look very similar to carrot tops.

Like so many other Umbelliferaes, Lomatium **resembles its poisonous relative, *Hemlock Parsley*.**

In the U.S. Northern Rockies, *Lomatium dissectum* is the largest member of its genus. **It can grow to 40" in height, on sturdy, hairless, hollow stems.**

The basal leaves of the plant are pinnately divided, petiolate, and are well described as *feathery* **in appearance; much like a fern, but with delicate carrot-like leaflets.** The leaves that grow directly from the stem of the plant are sparse

146

Lomatium

(sometimes absent) and much smaller, with short petioles (leaf stems).

Flowers are yellow and are presented in terminate umbels, 2"-5" across, that look like uniform clusters of yellow buttons.

The root consists of a well defined and often large taproot, which may have several crowns from which the aerial parts grow upward. The root bleeds a sticky, whitish sap when cut, particularly during spring. This gooey substance gives the root a unique pungency that smells like extremely strong-smelling celery or carrot, but with an added earthy overtone. Once you accurately identify this herb, you can practically identify it with a blindfold on.

Poison Hemlock, on the other hand, has an unpleasant, musty, dead odor about it.

Seeds are flat, oval, about ¼" long (large compared to poisonous look-alikes), and paper-like in texture *(see Fig. 4.3).*

HABITAT

Lomatium is a dryland plant that grows on steep, rocky hillsides, whereas Poison Hemlock (*Conium maculatum*) and its other toxic cousins are *usually* found in consistently moist, rich soil; seldom more than fifty feet from a water source, although I have recently been informed of instances where *Conium* and *Lomatium* were seen growing side-by-side.

Lomatium is frequently found growing in rockslides where the plants' roots are inhumed beneath a twelve inch layer of loose shale. It is not uncommon to find it growing directly out of the niches and fissures of vertical cliffs.

It is found most frequently at elevations between 2500' and about 6000'.

ACTIONS

Lomatium was used extensively as food and medicine by the Blackfeet and other tribes. It was commonly prescribed by

Lomatium

American physicians and pharmacists as an antiviral before the advent of vaccines and allopathic remedies. Recent studies have confirmed that Lomatium has an ability to kill forms of influenza virus, especially those that infect the respiratory tract. With the current global stew pot of new viruses, Lomatium may be re-entering the limelight of western medicine.

Lomatium also has other antimicrobial and immuno-stimulating qualities.

Fig. 4.3 The ripe seeds of Lomatium are distinctively different than those of its poisonous relative, Poison Hemlock (Conium maculatum). During the spring Lomatium produces yellow flowers. The flowers of Poison Hemlock are white.

Lomatium

PROPAGATION & GROWTH CHARACTERISTICS

Lomatium is a slow growing perennial that is difficult to effectively propagate. The plant increases in size through the production of root crowns, but distributes its population only by seed. Seeds are dispersed largely by gravity and/or run-off, with a low percentage of them ever accomplishing germination.

The plants do not translant well, as their roots tend to bleed profusely from even the smallest injury. This makes successful division of root crowns a poor-odds endeavor. But if you want this herb in your backyard don't despair... just keep trying. Each mature plant produces hundreds of seeds... gather a few from each of a variety of plants. Stratify them or plant them in the fall, covering the seeds with ¼" of soil in a dry, rocky location (preferably a hillside) in your garden. I have found that about 1 in 5 seeds will germinate, and that only about 1 in 5 of the seedlings will survive the first year. Give the seedlings plenty of water during their first year, then wean them off and let Nature take over.

GATHERING SEASON AND GENERAL GUIDELINES

Gather the mature roots after the foliage has died back and the flowers have gone to seed (usually late summer). Use a narrow, round nosed shovel or a geologist's hand pick to dig the often stubborn roots with minimum effort and impact. If any seeds remain on top of the dried stems, plant a few at the exact spot from which the root was dug, then scatter the rest in a manner that replicates natural process as closely as possible...

Wear good footwear and plan your approach. Avoid loose rocks and unstable slide areas altogether... human feet are poorly designed for this kind of terrain and will cause unnecessary impact, regardless of a $300.00 pair of mountain boots.

Gather conservatively and as infrequently as possible from multiple sites, bearing in mind that the roots you pull may be 7 or more years old. Monitor your impact and the propagation characteristics of each stand carefully. Keep

149

Lomatium

accurate records of your observations, and allow each stand to rest for a couple of years before you impact it again.

PARTS USED
The root.

CARE AFTER GATHERING
We prefer to tincture the fresh root, but the dried root can be used as well. Brush excess dirt from the freshly dug roots (do not wash them, or you are inviting mold) and cut them twice, lengthwise. The roots can then be dried in an open paper bag, or chopped down farthur for use in tinctures. Store dried roots *after they are completely dried* in a glass container; away from light. The dried root will remain in quality condition for six months or more. Tinctures will last forever, and eliminate any risk of spoilage and waste. TINCTURE FRESH ROOT: 1:2 Ratio; 70% alcohol. DRIED ROOT: 1:5 Ratio; 70% alcohol.

COMMON COMPANION HERBS
Balsamroot, Alumroot, Penstemon, Yarrow...

PLANT/ANIMAL INTERDEPENDENCE
Lomatium is often found as the predominant, if not the only plant on very steep hillsides. The large taproot is instrumental in erosion control, and often serves as a sort of rock dam in slide areas. This function becomes obvious once you have experienced a small rockslide while pulling a large root.

The yellow flowers are important pollinator-attractors, and the upper plant and roots are sometimes eaten by bears, bighorn sheep, and other large animals.

IMPACT CONSIDERATIONS
Consumer demands, habitat vulnerability, and the finicky, slow-growing characteristics of Lomatium warrants a high rating on the Impact Level scale.

In much of the dry, steep canyon country of East-

Lomatium

Central Idaho where Lomatium naturally flourishes, the plants have become scarce, and I have recently been told that they are now listed as "rare" in that state. I have also heard that it is scarce in New Mexico and Colorado. As the antiviral qualities of the plant become more widely recognized within the expanding herb market, one can only assume that more and more plants will be disappearing.

Lomatium is a valuable, *specialty herb* that should be used sparingly and specifically as a respiratory antiviral. Other effective and less irritating alternatives exist for other uses. **One large root will make enough tincture to last through several flu seasons... so gather it conservatively.**

There seems to be a general concensus among wildcrafters that the harvest of Lomatium should be kept to the bottom of hillside stands... the theory being that the stand is naturally maintained by the distribution of seeds from the upslope plants. Simple and true enough, but we should not overlook the variables. What about the *next* wildcrafter that gathers from the bottom of the same stand? And then what about the next one after that? *Where did the bottom of the stand used to be?*... What kind of condition are the upslope, mother plants in?... These are a few questions you should be asking yourself prior to impacting a stand.

Wear the right footwear and use good equipment to minimize habitat damage, **and try seeding this herb into your home garden. The wild plants could use a rest.**

Get to know the stands in your bioregion well, and keep in touch with them. Learn their needs and characteristics, and try to work within *their* abilities to provide.

PHOTO REFERENCES
Plants of the Northwest, Hitchcock (University of Washington Press – for line drawings)

TECHNICAL REFERENCES
Herbal Materia Medica, Michael Moore

Lomatium

Medicinal Plants of the Pacific West, Michael Moore
Edible and Medicinal Plants of the Rocky Mountains and Neighbouring Territories, Terry Willard, Ph.D. (photo *is not Lomatium dissectum,* but another species of *Lomatium*)
Quick Reference - Medicinal Plants of the Northern Rockies, Mary Wulff-Tilford

Check with your local herbarium or find someone who can show you this plant. A reference to the vascular plants of your area is likely to have line drawings of Lomatium. Oddly enough, few photo references are available for this time-proven herb.

STAND LOCATIONS

Date of Discovery	Location and Description of Stand	Site Record #

Motherwort

Leonurus cardiaca   Labiatae

IMPACT LEVEL. 2

OTHER NAMES
Lion's Ear, Leonurus.

DESCRIPTION
Motherwort is a unique Mint... it has the square stem and opposite leaf characteristics that are common to its family, but this is where obvious similarities stop.

It is large for a Mint, growing to as much as five feet in height on several erect stems. **Leaves are distinctively shaped, and reminiscent of a human hand with fingers spread wide open. The 1"–4" wide leaves are coarsely and sharply toothed, with the margins of the upper division reaching nearly to the midrib of the leaf.** The leaves grow directly off of the stem, and are progressively smaller and less toothed toward the top of the plant.

The flowers are small, pale pink, and presented in dense, whorled clusters at the axils of the upper leaves. Each of the tiny flowers has white hairs on its upper lip. The flower clusters will eventually develop into clusters of very sharp, hooked burrs.

The roots of the plant are in the form of fibrous, short rhizomes.

This plant is easy to recognize once you have been introduced to it. The unique leaf pattern of Motherwort makes it conspicuous, even when it is growing among a dense proliferation of other plants.

Motherwort

HABITAT
Motherwort is an Asian import, and its habitat in our country is difficult to define. It is usually found growing in prolific patches, but the stands are sporadically distributed across North America. It is common to find a dense stand of Motherwort growing within a one square mile area, and not a single plant within a radius of several hundred miles.

Its choice of habitat is as varied as its choice of geography. Although Motherwort prefers shady areas with evenly moist, rich soil, it is sometimes found in areas that are quite the opposite. It's rather fickle about its choice of elevation too, and can be found anywhere from about 1500' to nearly 8000' in the Mountain Northwest.

ACTIONS
A mild vasodilator, antispasmodic, cardiac tonic, diuretic, laxative, and sedative.

Motherwort has a long Chinese and Western history as an effective remedy for the discomforts of menstruation and PMS.

PROPAGATION & GROWTH CHARACTERISTICS
Motherwort is a perennial that reproduces from seed and by rhizome. It can be established in the herb garden if the seeds or root cuttings are kept continually moist throughout germination and early growth. For best results put the plants in compost-rich soil with a fairly neutral pH.

In its natural habitat, seeds are distributed by gravity and by passing animals that pick up the hooked burrs.

GATHERING SEASON AND GENERAL GUIDELINES
Gather Motherwort at the beginning of its bloom period; just before the flower buds open (anywhere from June to September).

Avoid gathering from areas where the soil is soft or very wet; the short, somewhat shallow rhizomes are vulnerable to compression injury. Gather from the periphery

Motherwort

of healthy stands, utilizing deer trails and other established avenues wherever possible.

Cut the stems diagonally, 2"-3" above ground level, with sharp clippers. The diagonal cut will help prevent the introduction of molds, fungus, or other organisms that may eventually infect and kill the root.

PARTS USED
All above-ground parts.

CARE AFTER GATHERING
Motherwort can be dried and used a short time later in tea, or it can be tinctured. We prefer tincture, as this assures optimum release of plant constituents and eliminates the shelf life dilemma.

If you choose to dry the herb, lay it out loosely on butcher paper or a non-metallic screen. Keep it away from light, allow for plenty of air circulation and rearrange it frequently to prevent molding. The properly dried and stored herb will remain in quality condition for only a very short period, so gather very conservatively and plan on tincturing whatever you do not use.

The fresh, flowering herb is best for tincturing. FRESH HERB TINCTURE: 1:2 Ratio; DRIED HERB: 1:5 Ratio; either/or with 60% alcohol.

COMMON COMPANION HERBS
Stinging Nettle, Burdock, Cleavers, False Solomon's Seal, Angelica, Catnip...

PLANT/ANIMAL INTERDEPENDENCE
Motherwort's interdependent roles vary according to its habitat, but some of its functions are well-defined.

Motherwort is an effective cover plant for insects, amphibians, reptiles, rodents, and other small animals. Its green, leafy structure breaks down readily after fall dieback and is particularly rich in calcium... a mineral that is as critical

Motherwort

to plants as it is to us.

The flowers attract pollinators from a level that is often above surrounding growth. This means that the plant serves as an advertiser for its companions; drawing the attention of bees and other insects that might otherwise pass over inconspicuous ground-huggers, such as Rattlesnake Plantain or low growing False Solomon's Seal. This kind of interdependent function can be particularly important within habitats that are subjected to frequent, radical climatic changes. The climatic variance possibilities in Western Montana present a good example... it is not uncommon to have 90 degree sunshine one day and frost the next. This puts enormous stress upon plants, particularly during their reproductive cycle, and requires a close cooperation within the plant community to assure that everybody has a chance to flourish. Tall plants, like Motherwort, hasten the opportunity seeking bee to its clients-in-need.

IMPACT CONSIDERATIONS

The sporadic nature of Motherwort's range raises the issue of over-harvest in areas where demand for the plant is high. A large stand of this plant can draw wildcrafters from miles around, and extra-bioregional wildcrafting generally involves a high level of impact ignorance. Even the bioregional herbalist is likely to find impact planning difficult in an area that is harvested by people from far away.

Keep close tabs on the stands in your area, and communicate with any other wildcrafters you may encounter. Take a head count. Post a sign, work with forest management authorities... camp on the trail if necessary. As herbalists we often hear the term *networking*. Lets take networking beyond the confines of marketing and into the natural realm, where it is needed to maintain the well-being of our plant allies.

Micro-ecosystems that are repeatedly impacted by ignorant, uncaring *or* caring wildcrafters are in grave danger.

Motherwort

PHOTO REFERENCES
The New Age Herbalist, Richard Mabey
Peterson Field Guides, Eastern/Central Medicinal Plants, Foster & Duke
Magic and Medicine of Plants, Reader's Digest Books

TECHNICAL REFERENCES
Menopausal Years, (Wise Woman Ways series), Susun S. Weed
The Holistic Herbal, David Hoffmann
Medicinal Plants of the Mountain West, Michael Moore
Quick Reference - Medicinal Plants of the Northern Rockies, Mary Wulff-Tilford

STAND LOCATIONS

Date of Discovery	Location and Description of Stand	Site Record #

Mullein

Verbascum thapsus   Scrophulariaceae

IMPACT LEVEL: 2

OTHER NAMES
Velvet Plant, Candle Leaf, Indian Tobacco, Blanket Leaf, Common Mullein.

DESCRIPTION
Mullein is a common and well-known weed that is recognized by its large, fuzzy leaves and its tall, flowering central stalk.

The leaves of Mullein are large (up to 16" long), broadly lance-shaped, and are **covered with a distinctive abundance of fuzz** that gives the plant a velvety texture. The plant grows a rosette of basal leaves during the first year of growth, and does not produce its sturdy, erect, central stalk until the second year.

During the second year the central stalk may grow as high as six feet, producing **a terminal cob-like cluster of yellow flowers.** The leaves of the main stem are much smaller than the basal leaves, and progressively reduce in size toward the top of the plant.

HABITAT
Mullein is an Earth-regenerator plant that is common to previously burned areas, roadsides, vacant lots, and other disturbed areas. It is widely regarded among farmers, ranchers, and gardeners as a troublesome weed.

Mullein can be found throughout North America, growing in just about any type of soil, at just about any elevation below timberline.

Mullein

ACTIONS

Expectorant, vulnerary, demulcent, diuretic. Mullein is useful as a cough remedy and in the treatment of earaches. The root is said to be useful for the treatment of bladder incontinence.

PROPAGATION & GROWTH CHARACTERISTICS *N O*

Mullein is a very efficient biennial. The long, terminal flower heads develop a multitude of capsules, each containing several tiny seeds. One plant will produce thousands upon thousands of seeds that are freely distributed when the dry flowerhead is shaken by wind or bumped by a passerby.

Mullein is not particular about soil. It prefers full sun but will tolerate partial shade. It is very cold hardy and drought resistant.

Although it is an easy plant to introduce into the herb garden, I don't recommend it unless you intend to harvest the herb prior to its maturity. If allowed to go to seed, you will likely be invaded, and seeds can remain viable in the soil for quite some time.

GATHERING SEASON AND GENERAL GUIDELINES ✓

Mullein leaves can be gathered anytime, but mid-season (May-August) leaves are generally in top condition.

Gather flowers and/or flowering tops when the buds are about half way open. Some herbalists insist upon the tedious task of picking off each individual flower, as opposed to cutting off the entire flowering top. The latter is much easier and produces fine medicines, but the plucked buds produce a prettier oil. I suppose it's a matter of how reverent you are to the Art of Zen and the Harvest of Mullein.

The root should be dug during its first year of growth. Since the plant is biennial, roots die and dry up after the bloom cycle.

Mullein

PARTS USED ✓
Flowers, flowering tops, or the leaves.

✓ **CARE AFTER GATHERING**
Leaves can be dried on a non-metallic surface, or tied into small bouquets (no more than 1" at the base) and hung in an airy place, away from light. Unlike most dryland plants, Mullein seems to be very vulnerable to mold while it dries, so watch it closely and rearrange it frequently. The dried leaves will keep for up to six months, if stored properly.

The flowers and flowering tops make an excellent ear oil if used fresh. The active constituents are contained in a dark, tarry substance that one can observe by picking apart the flower heads. This substance loses its potency as it dries.

Cut the "flower cobs" into small pieces and/or put the flower buds into a jar and cover with enough olive oil to make at least a ½" layer above the herb. It is very important that the herb remains submerged, otherwise the oil and herb will spoil. Weigh the herb down with a non-metal object if necessary. Seal the jar and allow it to sit for about one month, then strain it through a jelly bag.

✓ TINCTURE FRESH FLOWERS: 1:5 Ratio; 60% alcohol. LEAVES AND/OR ROOT: 1:2 Ratio, 60% alcohol.

COMMON COMPANION HERBS
Fireweed, Oregon Grape, Burdock, Dandelion, Chickweed, Yarrow...

PLANT/ANIMAL INTERDEPENDENCE
Although not a favorite forage source, Mullein often stands as the first source of small animal habitat in damaged areas. Mullein's stout taproot is effective in controlling erosion and breaking up compacted soil in areas where other plants have not yet recovered from fire or other impact. The tall, cob-like yellow flowers serve to reintroduce pollinators as well. Birds sometimes feed upon the ripe seed heads.

Mullein

IMPACT CONSIDERATIONS

Although Mullein is profusely abundant, I have rated it at "2" on the Impact Level scale because of its well-defined and critical role as an Earth-regenerator.

In areas where Mullein is busy at habitat repairs, gathering roots would serve to compound the previous impact. Leave these healing habitats alone and let Mullein do its job. It is an abundant plant that can be gathered from areas where its role is not as urgently critical.

Since this plant is viewed as *a noxious weed* (a term that must be common on the bathroom walls of the USDA), the wildcrafter should always suspect the introduction of herbicides. Do not gather this herb from cultivated areas... such as the front lawn of your local extension agent.

PHOTO REFERENCES

Weeds of the West, The Western Society of Weed Science

The New Age Herbalist, Richard Mabey (also contains technical info.)

Magic and Medicine of Plants, Reader's Digest Books (also contains technical info.)

Northwest Weeds, Ronald J. Taylor

TECHNICAL REFERENCES

The Holistic Herbal, David Hoffmann

Medicinal Plants of the Mountain West, Michael Moore

Quick Reference - Medicinal Plants of the Northern Rockies, Mary Wulff-Tilford

A Modern Herbal, Mrs. M. Grieve

The Herb Book, John Lust

Mullein

STAND LOCATIONS

Date of Discovery	Location and Description of Stand	Site Record #

Field Notes

Oregon Grape

Mahonia (Berberis) repens   Berberidaceae

IMPACT LEVEL 2

OTHER NAMES
Holly Grape, Mountain Grape Root, Mountain Holly.

DESCRIPTION
Three varieties of Oregon Grape are found in the Mountain Northwest: *Mahonia repens; M. nervosa;* and *M. aquifolium.* Of the three, *M. repens* is most common and the smallest.

M. nervosa is very similar to *M. repens,* but it is generally larger and has narrower, more lanceolate leaves.

The *aquifolium* species is a tall shrub that is frequently used in the floral industry as a bouquet filler. It is primarily found in the coastal forests of Oregon and Washington.

All three varieties are medicinally useful, but *M. repens* is considered a slightly more potent medicine than its cousins. It is the variety that is most frequently used by herbalists, and is the one this outline focuses upon.

Oregon Grape is a low-growing, evergreen shrub that rarely grows above 12". The plant originates from long rhizomes, sending up woody stems that bear **Holly-like leaves. The leaves are pinnately divided, consisting of 3-7 ovate to broadly lance-shaped leaflets. Leaflets are 1"-2" long and have very sharp spines along their edges. The upper surfaces of the leaves are glossy and darker in color than the undersides.** The leaves turn to predominantly red autumn colors during the fall.

The flowers of Oregon Grape are yellow, and grow in terminate racemes. These racemes later develop purplish-blue

163

Oregon Grape

berries that look like miniature grapes. The edible berries are juicy... and quite sour.

The root of Oregon Grape is strong and woody, with inner tissue that is distinctively yellow.

√ HABITAT

Oregon Grape is common throughout the Mountain West, with the exception of Southern California.

It prefers dry to moderately moist coniferous woodlands, from about 2500' to around timberline.

√ ACTIONS

This plant contains *berberine*, a bitter alkaloid that gives the roots their yellow color and a usefulness as a digestive tonic. It has an old reputation as a "blood purifier"; acting as a liver stimulant. It also possesses antipyretic, laxative, and antibacterial qualities.

√ PROPAGATION & GROWTH CHARACTERISTICS

Oregon Grape is a rhizomatous perennial that is frequently found growing in large, ground-hugging colonies. One rhizome can extend for several yards, sending up a proliferation of offshoots along its length. The plant also reproduces by seeds which are contained within the juicy berries. The seeds are small and very hard, and are widely distributed after passing through the digestive tracts of birds, bears, and herbivores.

Root cuttings can be established in the herb garden if kept evenly moist throughout early growth. Seeds can be started by mashing the ripe berries into pulp and then freezing (stratify) the whole mess. Then thaw the mash, strain out the seeds, and plant ¼" deep in the herb garden.

√ GATHERING SEASON AND GENERAL GUIDELINES

Oregon Grape can be dug anytime, but fall roots are slightly more potent and can be collected after the plant has dropped its seeds. Collect the plant by grasping the main stem

Oregon Grape

just above ground level. Pull *slowly* and steadily upward... the strong rhizomes will begin to come up like a shoelace. When you have exposed a foot or so of root, or if you meet alot of resistance, clip the root with a sharp pair of pruning shears.

PARTS USED
Primarily the root, but the above-ground portions of the plant contain valuable quantities of medicinal constituents as well and should not be wasted.
The roots of this plant make a beautiful goldenrod-yellow dye. It was used extensively by early peoples for this purpose.
With ample quantities of sugar, the berries make a good jelly or wine.

CARE AFTER GATHERING
The roots and aerial parts can be dried in a paper bag for use in infusions. The fresh herb can be tinctured immediately. FRESH HERB TINCTURE: 1:2 Ratio; DRIED HERB: 1:5 ratio... either/or with 50% (100 proof) alcohol.

COMMON COMPANION HERBS
Arnica, Yarrow, Bee Balm, False Solomon's Seal, Uva-Ursi, Balsamroot, Valerian...

PLANT/ANIMAL INTERDEPENDENCE
The rhizomatous nature of this plant makes it an effective soil aerator and erosion control agent. The late-producing berries and sometimes the leaves are browsed upon by deer, elk, moose, bears and the limitless assortment of rodents.

IMPACT CONSIDERATIONS
Although Oregon Grape is more resilient to the effects of soil compaction than many other rhizomatous plants, we must still take into account the shallow, horizontal nature of its roots. Although the largest plants are found in moist, soft

Oregon Grape

soils where shade prevails, the strongest roots come from sunny locations and dry, rocky soil. This is true of most root herbs... hot, dry, stressed-out plants retain higher concentrations of volatile oils in order to survive the elements. Gather from areas where soil compression will not be a problem, avoiding deep compost areas and moist, easily compacted soils. Never gather immediately after a period of precipitation and always wear soft footwear when gathering rhizomatous herbs.

Unless it's berries that you're after, leave the fruits for our animal companions. If you are gathering the berries gather conservatively, bearing in mind that they represent one of the last forage fruits available before the hardships of winter.

PHOTO REFERENCES

Forest Wildflowers, Dr. Dee Strickler

The New Age Herbalist, Richard Mabey (photo of *M. aquifolium*)

The Audubon Society Field Guide to North American Wildflowers, Richard Spellenberg

Nature Bound Pocket Field Guide, Ron Dawson

TECHNICAL REFERENCES

Medicinal Plants of the Pacific West, Michael Moore

The Holistic Herbal, David Hoffmann (listed as "Mountain Grape")

The Male Herbal, James Green

Herbal Healing for Women, Rosemary Gladstar

Edible and Medicinal Plants of the Rocky Mountains and Neighbouring Territories, Terry Willard, Ph.D. (also has a good photo)

Rodale's Illustrated Encyclopedia of Herbs, Rodale

Quick Reference - Medicinal Plants of the Northern Rockies, Mary Wulff-Tilford

Oregon Grape

STAND LOCATIONS

Date of Discovery	Location and Description of Stand	Site Record #

Field Notes

Osha'

Ligusticum spp.   Umbelliferae

IMPACT LEVEL: 3

OTHER NAMES
Porter's Lovage, Bear Medicine, Licorice-root, Canby's Lovage.

DESCRIPTION
Osha' is another member of the Carrot/Parsley Family with a frightening resemblance to its **poisonous relatives, Water Hemlock and Poison Hemlock. Osha' is very difficult for the untrained herbalist to differentiate from these plants, and I strongly discourage harvest by anyone who is not intimately familiar with them.**

Like other Umbelliferaes, Osha' presents umbrella-like, terminate flowcr clusters. Flowers are white to pinkish in color and are borne in one to a few umbels.

The leaves of Osha' are pinnately divided into one to four pairs, are up to 8" long, and depending upon the species, resemble the leaves of carrots or ferns. Where I live in Western Montana, *Ligusticum canbyi* is the predominant species, and it has a leaf that reminds me of the ferns that are commonly used by florists.

Plants grow anywhere from 4" to 36" tall (depending upon species and conditions), the stems are hollow and stout, and sometimes have purple splotches that give them a bruised appearance. Despite some claims that these splotches identify an Umbelliferae as one that is poisonous, I have seen this characteristic in *Angelica, Cow Parsnip,* and Osha' as well... in other words it is not a reliable identification characteristic.

Perhaps the best identifying characteristics of Osha' are its odor and the nature of its taproot. Osha' root smells like

168

Osha'

spicy celery (and once identification is positive, you will find that it tastes that way too). The root is proportionately large, brown, and *has dead leaf material around and near its crown, giving it a hairy appearance.*

The root of Poison Hemlock and other poisonous relatives have a dead odor about them, or little odor at all. The roots of Poison Hemlock are generally smaller, stringy or poorly defined as taproots. *They do not have the brown, hairy appearance about their crowns.*

HABITAT

Osha's habitat does not really help the herbalist in its identification, as it likes the same wet, mountain meadows that its poisonous relatives inhabit. Although Osha' is reputed as a high altitude plant that grows at elevations above the limits of Poison Hemlock. **This old guideline is unreliable.** The elevations at which Osha' can be found are much lower at the northern latitudes of the plant's range. For example... in the southern half of the Rockies, Osha' is seldom found below 8000'. In the northern Rockies it is commonly found as low as 5000'. To compound the identification problem furthur, **Poison Hemlock** is commonly found at elevations as high as 9500'.

Osha' requires a continuous source of moisture and prefers shady to partly sunny locations... again like its poisonous cousin.

Varied species of Osha' are found in montaine forests throughout the Mountain West.

ACTIONS

Antiviral, expectorant, diaphoretic, anesthetic to the throat. Osha' is a very effective and time-proven medicine that was used extensively by early peoples and is still popular today. It is particularly useful in the treatment of upper respiratory infections.

Osha'

PROPAGATION & GROWTH CHARACTERISTICS
Osha' is a perennial that reproduces by seed. It is very finicky about where it will grow, and is nearly impossible to transplant or start from seed in the garden. This plant is best left to reproduce naturally in its natural environment.

GATHERING SEASON AND GENERAL GUIDELINES
Osha' should be gathered after the flowers have gone to seed but before the aerial parts die back, after which positive identification can be extremely difficult.

This plant is becoming compromised by market pressure and habitat damage, and should only be gathered if absolutely necessary.

Osha's soft, wet environment is particularly vulnerable to human impact, and stands should be approached with the utmost of care and planning. Roots should be dug very conservatively from only the healthiest stands. Impact monitoring and accurate record-keeping is a must if we are to insure the future of this wonderful plant.

PARTS USED
The root.

CARE AFTER GATHERING
Like all roots that are gathered from a moist environment, Osha' *is* susceptible to mold after it is gathered, but is not as vulnerable as other wet habitat roots (such as Angelica). This is due to Osha's unique and effective antimicrobial qualities. But taking into account the impact you have caused during the harvest of the root, added care is owed nevertheless. If you are not going to use the fresh roots immediately, lay them in the sun to dry quickly. The dark brown skin of the roots will hasten drying and will protect the inner tissues from the damaging effects of sunlight. The dried roots will keep in good condition for a year or more if stored in a sealed glass jar.

Osha' is effective when chewed fresh or dried, or when

170

Osha'

used in teas or tincture. Mary and I think that the tincture, made from fresh root, is best.
TINCTURE FRESH ROOT: 1:5 Ratio; 70% alcohol.

COMMON COMPANION HERBS
Angelica, Cleavers, False Solomon's Seal, Pyrola, Pipsissewa, Cow Parsnip, Stinging Nettles, Horsetail...

PLANT/ANIMAL INTERDEPENDENCE
Osha' is said to have earned the common name "Bear Medicine" through Native American observations of sick bears consuming and rolling in the plant. It is a very tasty herb and is frequently foraged upon by moose, deer, and other large mammals... I don't doubt that they use the plant medicinally as well.

The large taproot and perennial die-back of the plant benefits the soil structure of its habitat. The flowers act as pollinator-attractors, and are particularly important in areas where the plant is growing as the predominant flower in shady wetlands.

IMPACT CONSIDERATIONS
Perhaps it is good that Osha' looks so much like Poison Hemlock... if it didn't, its popularity may have wiped it out by now. Its special affinity to the upper respiratory system and its rich history have inflated consumer demand to levels well beyond the plant's natural ability to provide. Greed and careless impact have reduced populations of Osha' into isolated, high altitude stands in many areas of the West. Although some of these stands may still be profuse, the lessons of time have shown us that this plant requires special, renewed care and consideration in order to survive.

Osha' is intended by Nature to provide us and our animal companions with a solution to a very specific set of needs. It should only be gathered in the *presence* of these needs and *not in anticipation of them.* For preventative therapies, you might try *Balsamroot.* As an expectorant or

Osha'

sore throat remedy, you might consider *False Solomon's Seal, Red Root,* or *Hound's Tongue. Lomatium* is an effective antiviral for the respiratory tract... *Sage* serves well as a throat antiseptic.

Osha' needs a break.

PHOTO REFERENCES

Medicinal Plants of the Mountain West, Michael Moore (also for technical reference)

Vascular Plants of West-Central Montana, Klaus Lackschewitz (excellent line drawings)

Consult your local herbarium and/or vascular plant guides that are specific to your bioregion.

TECHNICAL REFERENCES

Edible and Medicinal Plants of the Rocky Mountains and Neighbouring Territories, Terry Willard, Ph.D.

Quick Reference - Medicinal Plants of the Northern Rockies, Mary Wulff-Tilford

STAND LOCATIONS

Date of Discovery	Location and Description of Stand	Site Record #

Penstemon

Penstemon spp.   Scrophulariaceae

IMPACT LEVEL: 2

OTHER NAMES
Beardstongue.

DESCRIPTION
Penstemon represents a very large genus... there are hundreds of species throughout the West. Although Penstemon is not a popular medicinal herb, it is useful and abundant, so it deserves consideration in light of the need to relieve other plant allies of some of our harvest impact.

The many species of Penstemon vary widely in color, but most familiar are the blue varieties. The flowers are axillary and grow off of the stalk. They have two upper and three lower lips; stamens consist of four which are fertile and one which is sterile, with the latter often having a hairy tip.

Leaves are opposite and generally glossy, and range in shape from narrowly lanceolate to ovate. Some have toothed margins, some are smooth.

Penstemon is well known by wildflower enthusiasts wherever they grow. If you are unsure in the identification of the species native to your bioregion, consult your neighbor or a field guide that is specific to your area (see PHOTO REFERENCES)

HABITAT
Penstemon is a dryland wildflower that is common to sunny hillsides and meadows up to about 8000'.

ACTIONS
A topical astringent. Pureed or juiced, Penstemon can

173

Penstemon

be infused in olive oil for a week or more and used as a general dressing for minor irritations of the skin, such as insect bites. It is also good for relieving swollen hemorrhoidal tissues. Penstemon oil is a good addition to an all-purpose salve.

PROPAGATION & GROWTH CHARACTERISTICS
Penstemon is a hardy perennial. Several varieties are available at your local nursery, and they are easy and attractive to grow in the herb garden. Here in Western Montana, Penstemon blooms in early to mid-June and is often still in color through August.

GATHERING SEASON AND GENERAL GUIDELINES
The plant should be gathered while in bloom. Clip the stems three inches or more above ground-level, taking care not to disturb the roots. Large plants can be pruned from the center growth with very little visual impact.
Always leave plenty of flowers for the bees and the appreciative passerby.

PARTS USED
Entire above-ground plant.

CARE AFTER GATHERING
Use this herb fresh. Chop the stems, leaves, and flowers into small pieces. Put the chopped herb in a blender, juicer, or food processor and cover with olive oil. Blend it down until it looks like some sort of salad dressing, then put it in an airtight jar and let it infuse for at least a week (a month is better). Then strain it off and you have a good topical oil.
For emergency field use, a poultice can be made by grinding the herb with some water or saliva... then apply it directly onto the affected area.

Penstemon

COMMON COMPANION HERBS
Balsamroot, Yarrow, Arnica, Oregon Grape, Mullein...

PLANT/ANIMAL INTERDEPENDENCE
Like all long-lived wildflowers, Penstemon's role as a pollinator-attractor is well-defined. This plant often remains in bloom long after its companions have died back, making it a soup kitchen for bees and other flower dependent organisms.

IMPACT CONSIDERATIONS
Penstemon is wildcrafted more frequently by bouquet enthusiasts than by herbalists, making vicarious impact a constant possibility. Check your local markets for any presence of floral wildcrafting... more than once I have seen wildflower bouquets adorning restaurant tables or in a bucket beside the supermarket checkstand.

Penstemon shares habitat with a variety of *noxious weeds*, such as Knapweed or Thistle. Bear in mind that herbicides are not particular, nor are the herbicidal maniacs that paint the hillsides with poison.

PHOTO REFERENCES
The Audubon Society Field Guide to North American Wildflowers, Richard Spellenberg
Forest Wildflowers, Dr. Dee Strickler
Peterson Field Guides – any of the wildflower series.

TECHNICAL REFERENCES
Medicinal Plants of the Mountain West, Michael Moore
Quick Reference - Medicinal Plants of the Northern Rockies, Mary Wulff-Tilford

Unfortunately, technical information about this herb is as scarce as its application!

Penstemon

STAND LOCATIONS

Date of Discovery	Location and Description of Stand	Site Record #

Field Notes

Pineapple-weed

Matricaria matricarioides   Compositae

IMPACT LEVEL: 1

OTHER NAMES
"Wild Chamomile".

DESCRIPTION
Pineapple-weed is a close relative of domestic German Chamomile (*Matricaria chamomilla*). It is very similar in odor, flavor, and appearance to this popular after dinner tea plant, with a few exceptions.

Pineapple-weed has small, bright yellow, conical flowerheads that are nearly identical to those of Chamomile, **except that they are completely absent of any white rays.** This gives the flowers an immature appearance, leading some to believe that they have found a runaway stand of domestic Chamomile when discovering the plant.

The leaf characteristics of Pineapple-weed also closely resemble those of Chamomile, with opposite, greatly divided leaves that extend from the many stems. Although the plant can grow in excess of one foot tall, it generally presents itself in lower-growing mats of 6" or less.

The most distinguishing characteristic of this plant is its pleasant pineapple-like odor, which is so pungent that the plant often *identifies itself* when it is stepped on.

HABITAT
Pineapple-weed is native to North America, and has been widely distributed at northern latitudes across the globe. It is a sun-loving plant common to disturbed areas, vacant lots, and at roadside. It seems to prefer constant abuse, and is often found in abundance at vehicle turnouts and in the middle of footpaths.

Pineapple-weed

Matricaria matricarioides

ACTIONS
    Pineapple-weed can be used in exactly the same manner as Chamomile and is every bit as enjoyable. It is antispasmodic to the digestive tract and a gentle sedative, relieving stomachaches and gas pains while soothing the nerves. Topically it is a mild but effective anti-inflammatory agent.

Pineapple-weed

PROPAGATION & GROWTH CHARACTERISTICS

Pineapple-weed is a vigorous annual that readily reseeds itself and spreads rapidly. Each plant produces an abundance of diminutive seeds that germinate with a high level of success. The plant requires well packed soil, and tends to do best where it is continually trampled down by people, livestock, and vehicles.

Although moist, shady, low-impact conditions generally yield plants that are more attractive to the eye, the stronger medicine and tastier tea comes from the parched, impact-stunted plants growing in the center of walkways.

Pineapple-weed is very easy to establish in the herb garden, but has a tendency to run rampant if left unchecked. We introduced a single plant, dug from a highway turnout, into the walkway in front of our cabin in 1991. The plant looked pitiful the first year and received last rites from us several times. Then the next year it completely surrounded the house! As I wrote this book in 1993, I was looking from my window across a lush, ¼ acre of Pineapple-weed...

Don't be shy if you decide to transplant this herb. Dig one up during early spring, then stomp it into a hole with the heel of your shoe. The soil around the roots should be as tightly compressed as possible.

GATHERING SEASON AND GENERAL GUIDELINES

Gather Pineapple-weed after the flowerheads have turned bright yellow, but while the plant is still green and in good condition. Pluck the flowerheads or pull the entire plant (all parts are useable). Although I doubt that your gathering will effect next year's stand, leave plenty of plants for reseeding anyway.

PARTS USED

Use the flowers for a pleasant tea; the whole plant for oil infusions.

Pineapple-weed

CARE AFTER GATHERING

Pineapple-weed can be used fresh, but the dried flowers yield a more enjoyable tea. To dry the flowers, spread them on butcher paper or a non-metallic screen. Keep in a dry, light-free environment and store in a glass jar or ziplock baggie *after the herb is completely dry.* The dried herb will keep for a year or more.

To make an oil infusion, wilt the plants for a day after gathering. Cut the herb into small pieces, put it into a glass jar, and cover with enough olive oil to emerse the herb with a ½" layer of extra oil. Seal the jar and let it stand for a month or so before straining through a coffee filter or jelly bag. An ounce or so of vitamin E oil can be added to the finished product as a preservative.

COMMON COMPANION HERBS

Yarrow, Mullein, Dandelion, Dock...

PLANT/ANIMAL INTERDEPENDENCE

Birds and countless other creatures feed upon the sweet flowerheads of this herb... my chickens and the resident grouse and pheasants love it.

Pineapple-weed's perseverance in high-traffic areas makes it an important agent in Nature's battle against erosion. It often provides cover for small animals in places where none would otherwise exist, such as along highway shoulders.

IMPACT CONSIDERATIONS

The natural abundance, sturdiness, and practical usefulness of this delightful herb should make it a primary resource in the EcoHerbalist's tea cabinet. It is a plentiful weed that Nature has evidently provided in proliferation for the purpose of enjoyment and healing. It is in no foreseeable danger from human impact, and should be used within the scope of its medicinal actions before a more impact-sensitive herb is employed.

Unfortunately, some people view this wonderful plant as

Pineapple-weed

a troublesome weed... beware of the possible introduction of herbicides before you harvest. Gather from pollutant-free locations, avoiding roadways and cultivated areas.

PHOTO REFERENCES
   Weeds of the West, The Western Society of Weed Science
   Discovering Wild Plants, Janice J. Schofield (also has good technical information)
   Northwest Weeds, Ronald J. Taylor

TECHNICAL REFERENCES
   Medicinal Plants of the Desert and Canyon West, Michael Moore
   Quick Reference - Medicinal Plants of the Northern Rockies, Mary Wulff-Tilford

   Refer to information about Chamomile and employ this herb in the same manner.

STAND LOCATIONS

Date of Discovery	Location and Description of Stand	Site Record #

Pipsissewa

Chimaphila spp.   Ericaceae

IMPACT LEVEL: 3

OTHER NAMES
Prince's Pine, King's Cure, Pine Tulip, Love-in-Winter, Bitter Wintergreen, Ground Holly, "Wintergreen".

DESCRIPTION
There are four varieties of *Chimaphila* in the Mountain West. All are very similar, with a few differences in size and leaf pattern. All are small plants, with *Chimaphila umbellata* being the largest at a maximum height of 12".

Chimaphila menziesii is very similar in appearance to *C. umbellata* but is generally smaller and more delicate in structure. The two are frequently found growing together. *Chimaphila maculata* is a resident of Utah, Nevada, and Arizona. It too is similar, except it has light spots on its leaves.

All three varieties are medicinally useful and can easily be identified by the characteristics that follow.

Pipsissewa is a rhizomatous plant that grows on erect stems, generally 3"-10" high. The stems are simple or sparsely branched, woody at the base, and extend from long rootstalks. **The leathery, dark green, 1" to 5" lanceolate leaves have fine to coarsely serrated margins and grow in whorls from the stems, giving the plants the appearance of miniature trees.**

Flowers range from almost white to dark pink and have five petals, presenting themselves in groups of 1 to 3 atop a leafless, central flower stalk. The berries are produced from the flower stalks and are globe-shaped; each containing several tiny seeds.

182

Pipsissewa

HABITAT

Pipsissewa is a coniferous forest plant that likes undisturbed, deeply composted, mossy areas. It is commonly found growing directly through thick mats of sphagnum moss and around fallen, decaying trees. It requires evenly moist, acidic soil and at least 50% shade. *Chimaphila species* ranges from the mountains of Southern California, Arizona, and New Mexico at elevations above 6000'; and northward through the Rockies, the Sierras, Cascades, and the northwest coastal ranges to Alaska. The elevations at which it can be found become much lower as one travels north. Here in Western Montana, Pipsissewa can be found from about 3500' to timberline.

ACTIONS

Pipsissewa is a disinfectant and astringent that is much milder and less irritating to digestive and urinary tracts than its relatives, Uva-ursi and Manzanita. It is used by herbalists for the treatment of urinary tract infections and inflammation of the kidneys. It also has diuretic and diaphoretic properties.

PROPAGATION & GROWTH CHARACTERISTICS

Pipsissewa is a slow growing perennial that reproduces largely from its creeping rhizomes, and to a lesser degree from its seed. Although some references profess that it can be successfully established from root cuttings, a large degree of this success remains to be seen. The habitat in which Pipsissewa flourishes is impossible to duplicate in the absence of Nature's intent, and the cutting of roots for the doubtful purpose of transplanting can prove detrimental to an entire colony of offshoot plants.

The slow growth characteristics and stable habitat requirements of this plant makes starting it from seed a long, often frustrating endeavor, but this remains your best option for propagation. To introduce Pipsissewa into the herb garden, try to duplicate natural habitat and processes as closely

Pipsissewa

as possible. Gather seed in the fall and plant immediately into a medium that closely resembles that of its origin. Elevation and climate must be considered as well, and the richly composted soil must be kept evenly moist (not *wet*) throughout early growth.

GATHERING SEASON AND GENERAL GUIDELINES
Although this herb is useful anytime, it is considerate to gather Pipsissewa after it has gone to seed in the fall. Clip the stems above ground-level, taking care not to disturb the horizontal roots.
Always wear soft footwear, and avoid stepping between the plants whenever possible. Try to gather from the periphery of large, healthy stands, keeping in mind that your entrance into the stand will likely result in compression damage to the vulnerable roots. Avoid walking into mossy or deeply composted soils, and *never* gather Pipsissewa immediately following rainy periods. Wait for dry weather, when the forest floor regains its resiliency.
Gather very conservatively, and expect long-term impact from your harvest.

PARTS USED
The entire aerial plant.

CARE AFTER GATHERING
Pipsissewa can be be used fresh or tinctured. To use fresh, boil a teaspoon of the chopped herb in one cup of water for twenty minutes or more and drink as a tea. The leaves and stem are not very water soluable, necessitating boiling instead of standard infusion. Another option for tea is to "pickle" the chopped herb before infusing. This entails wetting the chopped herb with a small amount of brandy or your favorite booze and letting it stand for an hour before steeping in near-boiling water. The booze will act as a solvent to break down the resiliency of the plant tissues.
Tincturing is our favorite option, as it eliminates waste

184

Pipsissewa

and assures indefinite shelflife and maximum potency. TINCTURE FRESH HERB: 1:2 ratio; 50% (100 proof) alcohol.

COMMON COMPANION HERBS
Wild Ginger, False Solomon's Seal, Coptis, Rattlesnake Plantain, Pyrola (see Impact Considerations).

PLANT/ANIMAL INTERDEPENDENCE
Like many rhizomatous, deep-forest plants, Pipsissewa plays an important role as a soil aerator. The long, horizontally crawling roots break-up the continuity of dense carbonaceous forest debris and allows the introduction of air, water, and organisms... the essential elements needed for the nourishment and production of soil and plant life.

IMPACT CONSIDERATIONS
Although the scope of existing and potential impact upon Pipsissewa throughout this century has been tremendous, most herbalists remain innocently but ignorantly unaware. The fact is, Pipsissewa is commercially wildcrafted for use as an ingredient in root beer and other carbonated beverages. A very reliable source has recently informed me that a large soft drink company is taking it out of the forests of Oregon and Washington by the *container load* (a "container" is what you see behind a semi-truck) with no regard for environmental impact. This sort of greed-driven impact, coupled with the delicate, slow-producing nature of the plant and it's habitat puts the need for a proactive approach toward impact reduction into clear perspective. Although Pipsissewa remains abundant in North America, the range of this plant is becoming more and more sporadic. Our collective appetite for liquid tooth-rot is no small contributing factor and should not be overlooked by the EcoHerbalist.

To compound the consumer issue, the pristine environment that Pipsissewa flourishes in is vanishing in the face of suburban development and a snowball of impact caused

185

Pipsissewa

by inconsiderate logging and free-range livestock grazing. The subsequent effects of a rapidly increasing number of recreational users is another source of Pipsissewa's survival hardship, and until wilderness enthusiasts become more aware and caring of their impact upon delicate forest ecosystems, stands of Pipsissewa will likely continue to be replaced by campsites and trampled down foot trails.

Nature has provided us with an abundant herbal ally that serves well as an alternative to Pipsissewa. *Pyrola species* is similar in pharmacology and identical in use, is more abundant and widespread, grows faster than Pipsissewa, and is currently in small commercial demand.

PLEASE REFER TO *PYROLA* BEFORE GATHERING PIPSISSEWA.

PHOTO REFERENCES
Magic and Medicine of Plants, Reader's Digest Books
Edible and Medicinal Plants of the Rocky Mountains and Neighbouring Territories, Terry Willard, Ph.D.

The Audubon Society Field Guide to North American Wildflowers, Richard Spellenberg (photo of the flower only)
Forest Wildflowers, Dr. Dee Strickler

TECHNICAL REFERENCES
Medicinal Plants of the Mountain West, Michael Moore
Rodale's Illustrated Encyclopedia of Herbs, Rodale
The Male Herbal, James Green
Natural Healing with Herbs, Humbart Santillo
The Herb Book, John Lust
A Modern Herbal, Mrs. M. Grieve

Pipsissewa

STAND LOCATIONS

Date of Discovery	Location and Description of Stand	Site Record #

Field Notes

Plantain

Plantago spp.   Plantaginaceae

IMPACT LEVEL: 1

OTHER NAMES
Common Plantain, English Plantain, Mexican Plantain, Indian-wheat, Lantin.

DESCRIPTION
Several species of Plantain are common and widespread in North America. *Plantago major* (Common Plantain) and *Plantago lanceolata* (English Plantain) are perhaps the most recognized.

This family of plants are characterized by their broadly ovate to lanceolate, ground-hugging leaves that have **distinctive parallel leaf veins and are quite fibrous.** The leaves range from smooth to wooly, and often grow so closely to the ground that they appear to be squashed down.

Flower stalks are stiff and void of any leaves, up to 12" tall, and extend above the plant in groups of one to several. The tiny, pale yellow-green flowers present as themselves terminate, sausage-shaped, 1"to 3" clusters on each stalk. The flowers positively identify the plant, distinguishing it from members of the Lily Family... many of which resemble Plantain when young.

The entire plant is very mucilaginous, and if rubbed between the fingers, the juice feels sticky-oily.

Once this plant is identified, it is easy to remember. It is a common "lawn weed" throughout North America, and is often found growing from the cracks in streets and sidewalks... consult your local lawn care center for what may be a creatively verbose description of the varieties in your area.

Plantain

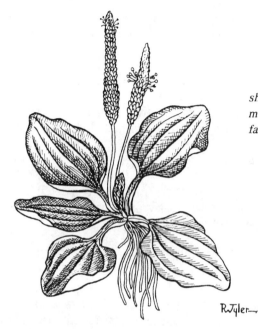

Plantains have sausage-shaped flowers, unlike members of the Lily family.

Plantago major

HABITAT
Plantain is common in disturbed areas such as roadways, grazed areas, pack animal stations and trails, lawns, and vacant lots. The tiny seeds travel well, and are often present in the "weed free" steer manure that you have probably already put into your lawn and garden.

It lives in a seemingly limitless diversity of habitats... from low desert to timberline across America and probably across the globe.

ACTIONS
Plantain is very effective as an emollient when used as a fresh poultice on insect bites, minor burns, and other skin

Plantain

irritations. The juice of the plant is useful to soothe intestinal irritations, hemorrhoids, and even stomach ulcers. The seeds, used fresh in tea, are said to act as an effective, lubricating laxative.

PROPAGATION & GROWTH CHARACTERISTICS

Plantains grow as perennials or annuals, depending on species, elevations, and climate. They reproduce largely by seed, and to a lesser extent from perennial division.

The introduction of this herb into the garden should be pursued only by genuine weed lovers, as it will likely find its way out of the flowerbeds and into pathways, driveways, and perhaps the neighbor's yard (you may have gotten it *from* there anyway). Plantain is not picky about soil quality, is very drought-tolerant, and prefers full sun over shade.

GATHERING SEASON AND GENERAL GUIDELINES

Plantain leaves and roots can be gathered anytime during green, healthy growth. **However, if you are not yet familiar with Plantain wait until the plant is flowering. Many members of the Lily Family can be mistaken for Plantain during early growth, and some of these mistakes could prove toxic. Once Plantain presents flowers, it is unmistakable.**

Gather Plantain by grasping the plant at its base and pulling. In dry soils, the aerial plant will often break off at ground-level. If you desire the root, use a ditch spade or hand trowel. For poultices and/or field use pluck off the leaves.

CARE AFTER GATHERING

This herb is best if used fresh. For bites, Stinging Nettle attacks, and first degree burns a first aid poultice can be quickly made by chewing up some leaves and applying the goo directly to the affected area. The plant is entirely edible and quite tasty aside from its tough fibers which make excellent cordage or thread material.

At home, a blender or juicer can be employed to make

Plantain

topical poultices or purees (juice if you have a *good* juicer) for internal uses.

COMMON COMPANION HERBS
Any variety of several masochistic, sun-loving herbs can be found alongside Plantain. These may include: *Pineapple-weed, Mullein, Dandelion, and Horehound.*

PLANT/ANIMAL INTERDEPENDENCE
Plantain serves as a "standby staple" for herbivores... it is seldom a primary forage but is usually available if needed. Its capability to survive drought and continual trampling make it an effective soil structure engineer. Plantain's roots, although not always as fibrous and tough as the leaves, are very effective in penetrating hardpan soils and preventing erosion in places such as road margins.

IMPACT CONSIDERATIONS
Although Plantain is profusely abundant from the Pacific to the Atlantic, the EcoHerbalist must remember that natural needs take precedence over ours in terms of dependency. This plant serves as an indicator of surrounding conditions. If a stand of Plantain appears to have been foraged upon, one should suspect that other sources of forage have been depleted. If the Plantain in your area appears to be unusually growth-stunted, then the less resilient plants in your area are probably suffering (*less resilient* usually means *everything else*). In either case, leave the Plantain for the animals and do without... or seek an alternative, such as *Penstemon* or *Pineapple-weed* (provided that they are not being eaten as well).
Since Plantain is often hated by herbicidal maniacs, beware of toxic introductions.

PHOTO REFERENCES
Weeds of the West, The Western Society of Weed Science

Plantain

Northwest Weeds, Ronald J. Taylor
The Audubon Society Field Guide to North American Wildflowers, Richard Spellenberg
The New Age Herbalist, Richard Mabey
Discovering Wild Plants, Janice J. Schofield

TECHNICAL REFERENCES
Medicinal Plants of the Mountain West, Michael Moore
Wise Woman Herbal for the Childbearing Years, Susun S. Weed
Out of the Earth, Simon Y. Mills
The Holistic Herbal, David Hoffmann
The Male Herbal, James Green
The Healing Herbs, Michael Castleman (see *Psyllium*)
The Herb Book, John Lust
Natural Healing with Herbs, Humbart Santillo
Quick Reference - Medicinal Plants of the Northern Rockies, Mary Wulff-Tilford

STAND LOCATIONS

Date of Discovery	Location and Description of Stand	Site Record #

192

Poplar

Populus spp.   Salicaceae

IMPACT LEVEL: 2

OTHER NAMES
Aspen, Quaking Aspen, Balsam Poplar, Cottonwood, "Balm of Gilead".

DESCRIPTION
Aspen, Poplar, and Black Cottonwood, and other members of *Populus* species are common to riparian habitats throughout North America. They can be characterized by their sharp-pointed, heart-shaped leaves that grow alternately on proportionately long leaf stems (petioles).

Poplars have gray, rough bark during maturity and smooth, whitish-green bark when young. Quaking Aspen *(Populus tremuloides)* has greenish, off-white bark throughout its maturity and is distinguishable by its showy presentation of contrasts within its habitat. In addition to the whitish bark that stands out from the surrounding flora, Quaking Aspen has broad leaves that "tremble" in even the slightest of breezes, adding contrasting elements of motion and a unique rustling sound to its character.

Poplars produce long, drooping catkins just prior to spring leaf growth. These catkins are sweet to the nose and tongue and sticky to the touch. Seeds are distributed by airborne tufts of white hairs that sometimes embark upon their reproductive ventures in dramatic profusion. Here in Montana, the airborne tufts sometimes mimic a springtime snowstorm!

If you are not familiar with Poplars, an easy way to introduce yourself is by visiting your local nursery. These attractive, fast-growing trees are very popular as landscaping

Poplar

ornamentals and adorn backyards and city streets everywhere.

Populus balsamifera (Balsam Poplar) - **Top**; *Populus tremuloides (Quaking Aspen)* - **Bottom**. *Petioles are proportionately long. Flowers are presented as drooping catkins. Male and Female catkins are on separate trees.*

Poplar

HABITAT

Wild stands of Poplar are common to stream banks, wet draws, and other riparian habitats from the low deserts to the upper rim of the subalpine zone. Their primary requirement for survival is a constant water source.

ACTIONS ✓

The primary action of Poplar is analgesic, used both topically and internally. Like other members of the Willow Family, Poplar contains varying amounts of *populin* and *salicin...* compounds that relate to early forms of aspirin.

Poplar also offers cathartic, diuretic, alterative, expectorant, nephritic, demulcent, and vulnerary qualities as well.

PROPAGATION & GROWTH CHARACTERISTICS

Poplars are deciduous trees that require a constant source of moisture... a stand of native Aspens or Cottonwoods is usually a reliable indicator of a shallow source of ground water.

The male and female catkins are borne on separate trees, so if you decide to plant a grove, be sure to get trees of both sexes.

These trees are a beautiful addition to the yard or pasture and are easy to establish from nursery stock.

GATHERING SEASON AND GENERAL GUIDELINES

Gather the young, sticky buds shortly after they appear in early to mid-spring. Gather conservatively from the branches that are within easy reach, and carry some rubbing alcohol with you to periodically clean the goo from your fingers, or you will soon find that you cannot release the buds from your grasp! Forget gloves... they become a sticky mess in no time.

Gather bark during the spring; when it separates easily from the smaller limbs. To remove the bark, make small incisions with a sharp knife, about 6" apart, on a limb that is

Poplar

within easy reach. **Be certain that the incisions do not extend over more than ¼ of the limb's circumference, or you may kill the limb.** After the incisions are made, make two more, lengthwise, to form an etched rectangle on the limb.
Now peel the rectangle off with your fingers... it should lift off easily. If it doesn't, chances are it's not springtime anymore, or the tree is suffering from a shortage of water.
If a gooey glob of pine pitch is available nearby, use it to bandage the wound you have caused... this will help to prevent infection (who says that trees aren't people?). A commercial brand of pruning compound will serve this purpose as well.

PARTS USED
Primarily the buds and inner bark. The buds are the most potent medicine and can be gathered with a minimal degree of impact on the tree.
➤ The green cambium layer (or inner bark) is the part which carries nutrients, water, and volatile oils to the leaves. It contains higher concentrations of active constituents than the dry outer bark, but not as high as those contained within the buds. The buds are not very water soluble though, and are best used in oils, ointments, and salves.

CARE AFTER GATHERING
If gathered early enough in the spring, the moist inner bark can be peeled away from the outer bark and dried by itself in paper bags or on butcher paper. This makes for an herb that has a higher potency-to-bulk ratio and is better tasting in teas. But if bark separation is impossible, dry it and use it anyway. The dried bark can be stored in an airtight container for a year or more.
The buds are best if used fresh.

PLANT/ANIMAL INTERDEPENDENCE
Poplars represent food, shelter, and nesting habitat for a wide variety of organisms... from pollinating insects and ants to ospreys, eagles and large mammals. I often see whitetail

Poplar

deer and moose browsing on the lower leaves and young branches, and during hard winters I have seen evidence of forage on the rich inner bark. Cottonwoods and Aspens are favored by beavers, who not only eat the trees but use the leftovers for construction.

IMPACT CONSIDERATIONS

Although a poor fuel wood, more and more *Populus* is ending up in the fireplace. In areas of Central and Eastern Montana, as well as many areas of the Plains States and the Midwest, Cottonwood remains as the primary source of winter heat. Although Poplars grow relatively fast, they cannot keep up with humanity's population growth, and in some areas large stands are shrinking quickly. Fortunately, this herb can be gathered with little or no impact on plant populations or stand quality... but care and foresight is still required.

PHOTO REFERENCES

The Audubon Society Field Guide to North American Wildflowers - Western Region, Elbert L. Little
Edible and Medicinal Plants of the Rocky Mountains and Neighbouring Territories, Terry Willard, Ph.D. (also has technical information)
Discovering Wild Plants, Janice J. Schofield (also has technical information)

TECHNICAL REFERENCES

Medicinal Plants of the Pacific West, Michael Moore
The Holistic Herbal, David Hoffmann
The Herb Book, John Lust
Peterson Field Guides - Eastern/Central Medicinal Plants, Foster & Duke
Rodale's Illustrated Encyclopedia of Herbs, Rodale
Quick Reference - Medicinal Plants of the Northern Rockies, Mary Wulff-Tilford

Poplar

STAND LOCATIONS

Date of Discovery	Location and Description of Stand	Site Record #

Field Notes

Pyrola

Pyrola spp.   Ericaceae

IMPACT LEVEL: 2

OTHER NAMES

Wintergreen, Alpine Wintergreen, Woodnymph, Sidebells, Frog's Reading Lamp, Bethlehem Star, Kidneyleaf.

DESCRIPTION

Several species of Pyrola inhabit coniferous forests across North America. One of the most common and widespread is *Pyrola secunda,* or "Sidebells Pyrola".

Most of the Pyrola gang can be identified by their **basal clusters of dark green, shiny, broadly lanceolate to ovate leaves that are generally on the smaller side of 3" wide.**

The terminate, 5-petalled flowers are presented on top of an unbranched, leafless, erect stalk, and range in color from white/whitish-green to varying shades of pink. The flowers grow in loosely arranged racemes, with the flowers of *Pyrola secunda* presenting themselves along only one side of the flowering stalk.

Pyrola is a rhizomatous perennial that is often found growing as dense "colonies" in shaded, moist woods. The broad leaves and creeping growth characteristics of this plant sometimes lead wildcrafters to believe that they have found a patch of Wild Ginger *(Asarum spp.).* When compared side-by-side, these two plants look quite different, with Wild Ginger having larger, broadly heart-shaped leaves. To eliminate *any* confusion between these two herbs, Wild Ginger *smells like ginger,* while Pyrola has little if any distinctive odor at all.

Pyrola

Pyrola species

HABITAT
Most Pyrolas live in shady coniferous forests, in soils that are generally high in wood compost. One exception is *P. grandiflora*, a large flowered inhabitant of Alaska and Western Canada that can also be found in dry forest clearings.

Pyrola

Pyrola is believed to have a symbiotic interdependency with wood-rotting varieties of fungus, and it is often found growing in shady, damp areas where the forest floor is thick with decomposing debris. This genus is widely distributed across the northern hemisphere, and is found in low lying riparian habitats and dense forests up to timberline.

ACTIONS
Pyrola is an excellent astringent and disinfectant that is especially useful in urinary tract infections. It is **pharmacologically very similar to its more heavily impacted family member, Pipsissewa,** and can be applied in exactly the same manner *(See Pipsissewa).*

PROPAGATION & GROWTH CHARACTERISTICS
Pyrola is a perennial that sends up offshoots from nodes on its creeping stems and roots. It also reproduces by seed. Unfortunately, this plant *does not transplant,* and is nearly impossible to start from seed. The natural habitat that Pyrola enjoys is one of incomprehensibly delicate symbiotic checks and balances that cannot be mixed up in a garden bucket. Like many of its companion herbs, Pyrola is a critically interdependent member of its biocommunity.
In spite of its unwillingness to be domesticated, Pyrola is very hardy within its environment and can survive several hard frosts before dying back.

GATHERING SEASON AND GENERAL GUIDELINES
Pyrola is useful anytime, but should be gathered after its reproduction cycle is complete; generally early fall.
Find a large patch that is easy to access and *cut* a leaf or two from several healthy plants. Avoid pulling the leaves... the roots of this plant are rather weak and can be damaged easily. Likewise, the spongy, compost-rich soil that Pyrola inhabits is easily compressed by human feet. Wear soft shoes and plan your approach carefully. Gather at the margins of a

Pyrola

footpath or well-used animal trail whenever possible. Visual impact is indicative of over-harvest.

PARTS USED
The leaves.

CARE AFTER GATHERING
Same as *Pipsissewa*.

COMMON COMPANION HERBS
Pipsissewa, Wild Ginger, Mints, Horsetail, Cleavers, Cow Parsnip, Angelica, False Solomon's Seal...

PLANT/ANIMAL INTERDEPENDENCE
Pyrola and its environment allows us to have an enlarged, humanly tangible look at how the the natural world around us *really* operates... if we allow ourselves to see.
The complexities involved in the interdependencies between plants, animals, fungi, an endless variety of microorganisms, *and* the biospherical and atmospherical elements of the Earth are far beyond human comprehension. When one *begins* to discover some of the minute but critically essential, unseen processes that occur within an ecosystem, one also begins to discover the arrogance and futility of trying to "manage" a forest. Plants such as Pyrola provide an outstanding beginning to an education into new levels of natural awareness. Here we can see how fungi and other microorganisms join with water and oxygen to break down the detritus into nutrient-rich soil with the assistance of an equally dependent, symbiotic organism: Pyrola. As we look deeper into this interdependent community, we see that Pyrola was introduced into the picture by yet another organism (perhaps through animal droppings), or by a natural occurence (such as rain run-off). After becoming established as a member of the forest floor community, Pyrola works as a liaison between its companion organisms and the elements. But here the interdependency deepens even more... Pyrola cannot maintain

Pyrola

its chores without the assistance of *more* organisms; pollinators and other members of the biocommunity (all of which are interdependent with one another as well) join the party. The interdependent continuum goes on and on. On beyond microscopic, cellular levels and into chemistry, quantum physics, and the unknown. And if *one* miniscule element is removed from the scenario, the entire community may die.

Here's some food for thought: when we take into consideration the simple fact that Pyrola is sometimes browsed upon by deer, elk, moose, and smaller herbivores in efforts to adjust our wildcrafting impacts accordingly, we are actually looking *beyond* the scope of most modern, mainstream "forest management" programs! Kinda puts "human intervention" into a different perspective, doesn't it?

IMPACT CONSIDERATIONS

Although this herb is plentiful and widespread, it lives in an environment that tends to be vulnerable to human impact. Gather this herb only as needed and focus its use upon its specialty... the urinary tract. For other applications you will likely find a more effective alternative.

Gather from multiple sites and monitor the short and long-term effects of your wildcrafting very closely. Never gather this herb in the presence of other human impact, such as trail construction, logging or cattle grazing unless the compound effects of such activities can be forecasted accurately. For example: gathering Pyrola from a stand that will fall to the construction of a new road next week is a good idea. However, gathering from the periphery of such areas may lead to vicarious impact when people using the road venture off into the woods.

Pyrola

PHOTO REFERENCES

The Audubon Society Field Guide to North American Wildflowers, Richard Spellenberg

Edible and Medicinal Plants of the Rocky Mountains and Neighbouring Territories, Terry Willard, Ph.D.

TECHNICAL REFERENCES

Medicinal Plants of the Mountain West, Michael Moore

Discovering Wild Plants, Janice J. Schofield (also contains good photos)

Quick Reference - Medicinal Plants of the Northern Rockies, Mary Wulff-Tilford

STAND LOCATIONS

Date of Discovery	Location and Description of Stand	Site Record #

Raspberry

Rubus spp   Rosaceae

IMPACT LEVEL: 2

OTHER NAMES
Red Raspberry, Black Raspberry, Blackcap, Thimbleberry.

DESCRIPTION
Raspberries are generally characterized by their thorny, trailing, biennial stems (or "canes") and the familiar red or black fruits.

The leaves are alternate in most species, and are divided into 3-5 broadly lance-shaped, ½"-3" long leaflets. Leaves may or may not have spiny petioles, and are borne off of the woody, yellowish to reddish-brown canes.

Flowers of most species are white and have five petals.

Rubus parvifloris (Thimbleberry) has leaves that are large (up to 6" long) and shaped much like those on maples. Stems are void of any spines, and the bright red fruits are borne from the ends of the stems in far less abundance than its neighboring Raspberries.

HABITAT
Raspberries are distributed across the northern hemisphere, with stands becoming somewhat more sporadic at the more southern latitudes. It is common to riparian areas, canyon bottoms, and moist woods; from low elevations to timberline, and is often found in irrigation and roadside ditches as well.

ACTIONS
A uterine astringent, diuretic, laxative, mild sedative.

Raspberry

Rubus idaeus

PROPAGATION & GROWTH CHARACTERISTICS
Like domesticated varieties, wild Raspberries produce long, often tangled biennial canes that produce fruit off of

Raspberry

second year growth. The fruits of wild Raspberry are generally much smaller than domesticated versions, but are otherwise essentially the same. Although Raspberry is often found growing as nearly impenetrable thickets in disturbed roadside areas and vacant lots, it tends do be difficult to establish from cuttings or transplants. Domesticated varieties should be obtained from the nursery for garden introduction.

Raspberries require acid soils, ample moisture, and plenty of potassium (potash). Although they grow well in shade, plants that are allowed full sun will likely produce alot more fruit.

GATHERING SEASON AND GENERAL GUIDELINES

For the strongest medicine and best tasting tea, gather leaves just as flowerbuds are forming in early spring. If you miss this harvest date the older leaves can still be used, provided they remain in good condition. Wear gloves and a long sleeved shirt to protect yourself from the prickly stems, and gather from the periphery of several different patches. Avoid entering the patches, as such ventures can not only be physically painful, but disruptive to a number of creatures that may be nested within the protective canes.

Gather fruits when they are ripe; in the same manner as the leaves.

PARTS USED

Primarily the leaves in tea; fruits for food use.

CARE AFTER GATHERING

Raspberry leaves should be used either fresh or *completely* dried. **Leaves temporarily develop toxic substances when they wilt.**

I prefer the dried leaves for tea, as they are more soluble and better tasting than fresh. To dry the leaves, spread them out on butcher paper or a non-metallic screen. Put them in a warm, dry, lightless place and stir them

Raspberry

frequently to prevent the development of mold. After the leaves are entirely brittle, store them in a glass jar. The dried herb will keep for a year or more if kept airtight and away from sunlight.

COMMON COMPANION HERBS
Stinging Nettle, Cleavers, Sweetroot, False Solomon's Seal, Burdock...

PLANT/ANIMAL INTERDEPENDENCE
As most would suspect, Raspberry fruit is relished by everything from mice to bears. Birds are particularly fond of the berries, with migratory flocks commonly returning to the same patches of the brambles year after year.

The dense, thorny entanglement of large stands provide protective cover and habitat for birds and small animals. In the streamside patches near my cabin, one is almost guaranteed to find occupied grouse nests throughout the spring and early summer months.

IMPACT CONSIDERATIONS
Although abundant enough to be considered a problem plant by many, Raspberry rates a "2" on the impact scale because of its well defined contributions to its biocommunity. It provides critical sources of habitat and food, and the removal of large stands would certainly have a profound effect on the biodiversity of its chosen environment.

Despite the benefits this plant offers to both humanity and our natural companions, many agencies and individuals have waged chemical warfare against it... check for the possible introduction of herbicides before you harvest, and keep in touch with your sources afterwards.

PHOTO REFERENCES
Discovering Wild Plants, Janice J. Schofield (also contains technical information)
The New Age Herbalist, Richard Mabey

Raspberry

Edible and Medicinal Plants of the Rocky Mountains and Neighbouring Territories, Terry Willard, Ph.D. (also technical information)

Magic and Medicine of Plants, Reader's Digest Books

TECHNICAL INFORMATION

Menopausal Years, Susun S. Weed
The Holistic Herbal, David Hoffmann
The Male Herbal, James Green
The Herb Book, John Lust
Medicinal Plants of the Mountain West, Michael Moore
Quick Reference - Medicinal Plants of the Northern Rockies, Mary Wulff-Tilford

STAND LOCATIONS

Date of Discovery	Location and Description of Stand	Site Record #

Rattlesnake Plantain

Goodyera oblongifolia   Orchidaceae

IMPACT LEVEL: 3

OTHER NAMES
Western Rattlesnake Plantain, Western Orchid, Netleaf Plantain, Peramium.

DESCRIPTION
Despite what this plant's common name implies, Rattlesnake Plantain is not at all related to Plantain *(Plantago spp.)*. In fact, it is not even a member of the same family. The common name reference between these two, separate herbs is based on a similarity in appearance; both Plantain and Rattlesnake Plantain grow in a flattened, ground-hugging rosette fashion. Both herbs are identical in medicinal application as well, with Plantain *(Plantago spp.)* as the better choice of the two in respect to abundance and widespread availability.

This profile of Rattlesnake Plantain is for the benefit of those urgently requiring the herb in a field situation. In instances where immediate application is not required or *Plantago* is readily available, I urge you to leave the less common Rattlesnake Plantain alone.

Rattlesnake Plantain grows as rosettes of fleshy, lanceolate leaves that are generally no larger than 3" long. The leaves have a yellowish midrib and mottling that gives them a webbed appearence.

Flowers are greenish-white, characteristic of the orchid family, and grow along one side of a leafless, central flower stalk.

Rattlesnake Plantain

HABITAT

Rattlesnake Plantain is at home in shady, heavily composted and sometimes mossy coniferous forests, from about 4000' to the upper limits of the subalpine zone. It ranges throughout the Mountain West, but becomes more sporadic at the southernmost latitudes.

ACTIONS

Same as *Plantain.*

GATHERING SEASON AND GENERAL GUIDELINES

Gather one or two leaves from multiple plants, anytime that they are in good condition.

PARTS USED

The leaves.

CARE AFTER GATHERING

Same as for *Plantain* (see Index)

IMPACT CONSIDERATIONS

Rattlesnake Plantain lives in an environment that is much more sensitive to impact than that of true Plantain *(Plantago spp.)*, and the plant itself is far less prolific than its common ally. Therefore, the employment of this herb should be limited to urgent applications only.

PHOTO REFERENCES

Peterson Field Guides - Eastern/Central Medicinal Plants, Foster & Duke (refers to the similar *G. pubescens* variety)

TECHNICAL REFERENCES

Medicinal Plants of the Mountain West, Michael Moore
Quick Reference - Medicinal Plants of the Northern Rockies, Mary Wulff-Tilford

Red Root

Ceanothus spp.   Rhamnaceae

IMPACT LEVEL: 2

OTHER NAMES
Buckbrush, Snow Brush, New Jersey Tea, Mountain Lilac, Evergreen Ceanothus, Shiny-leaf Ceanothus.

DESCRIPTION
Ceanothus represents a large, characteristically varied genus of shrubs. *Ceanothus velutinus* is widely distributed in the Mountain West, and is the one that is commonly recognized by herbalists. Many other species, including *Ceanothus arboreus, C. spinosis,* and *C. thyrisflorus* are characteristically similar (particularly in the leaves) but are larger and are mainly found in the coastal canyons and foothills of California, Oregon, Washington, and B.C..

For the purpose of practical simplicity, this profile will be focused upon *Ceanothus velutinus.*

Red Root is a spreading shrub, seldom reaching a height above 4'. **The ovate leaves are dark green with a shiny upper surface and a grayish, hairy surface beneath, and have a smooth but gummy texture. Each leaf has three distinctive veins originating basally.**

Twigs are yellowish-green.

The roots are strong and knotted, with inner bark that is characteristically red.

The flowers are presented in dense, yellowish-white clusters and are sweetly pungent.

HABITAT
Ceanothus velutinus is common to dry, south to west-facing mountain slopes. It often stands as the predominant

Red Root

shrub in its habitat, and can be found in abundance throughout the coastal ranges extending from B.C. to Southern California, and eastward from Oregon and Washington to the Dakotas.

ACTIONS
Lymphatic stimulant, astringent, tonic, antiseptic.

PROPAGATION & GROWTH CHARACTERISTICS
Red Root is a slow growing evergreen shrub that for all purposes cannot be transplanted. The roots of this plant are very strong and often quite thick, with an ability to slowly weave their way through hard, rocky subsoils. Some of the specimens I have *attempted* to dig seemed to be fused or imbedded into solid stone, making my efforts pointless in the absence of dynamite.

The seeds of this species are capable of lying dormant in the soil for up to two hundred years before germinating.

GATHERING SEASON AND GENERAL GUIDELINES
The roots and leaves can be gathered anytime, however the fall roots tend to contain higher levels of active constituents.

Using a round-nosed ditch spade, carefully expose some of the roots near the base of a healthy shrub. With a sharp pair of pruning shears, **cut no more than two of the smaller (1" or less) peripheral roots from the plant.** Contrary to common practices, there is no need to deliberately kill the plant by digging the entire root. After you have collected the root, cover the hole in and pack the soil down as firmly as you can. Include each specific shrub into your field notes, and monitor the shrubs closely for at least two years. If your gathering methods were successful, the shrubs will show an initial slowing of growth but will not die. If your impact does prove fatal, adjust your gathering accordingly.

Always try to gather the smallest, shallowest roots possible, and abandon your efforts whenever natural resistance dictates (ie., if you hit solid rock while digging, move to an

Red Root

easier plant). Always distribute your impact over several shrubs and multiple stands.

The leaves can be conservatively gathered with little effect upon the plant.

PARTS USED

The roots or leaves.

CARE AFTER GATHERING

The dried & chopped root or dried leaves can be used as an infusion as needed. Fresh leaves can be chewed for urgent relief of sore throats.

TINCTURE FRESH ROOT: 1:2; DRIED ROOT: 1:5, 50% alcohol.

The fresh root is best for tincturing. The dried root (chopped and dried in paper bags) can be kept for years if stored in airtight, lightless containers. The dried leaves will keep for about a year.

COMMON COMPANION HERBS

Spirea, Balsamroot, Lomatium, Valerian, Elder, Yarrow...

PLANT/ANIMAL INTERDEPENDENCE

Ceanothus species represents a major source of forage for deer, elk, and other herbivores. The pungent flowers are very attractive to bees and other pollinators, and the often dense stands of foliage is the home of an endless variety of wildlife.

On the subterranean level, Redroot has nodes along its roots that are host to nitrogen-fixing bacteria... an attribute that benefits all surrounding plantlife. The roots are also effective aerators, allowing the introduction of air and water into what may be an otherwise impervious layer of hardpan.

Red Root

IMPACT CONSIDERATIONS

In light of this plant's critical role as shelter and food source (for both animal and plant), and its very slow growth rate, Red Root should be gathered *very conservatively* and in cooperation with close monitoring. Although abundant, this plant and its many natural dependents deserve extra consideration.

PHOTO REFERENCES

The Audubon Society Field Guide to North American Trees, Elbert L. Little (photos are of different species that share very similar characteristics)

TECHNICAL REFERENCES

Medicinal Plants of the Pacific West, Michael Moore.
The Herb Book, John Lust (under "New Jersey Tea")
A Modern Herbal, Mrs. M. Grieve
Rodale's Illustrated Encyclopedia of Herbs, Rodale ("New Jersey Tea")
Quick Reference - Medicinal Plants of the Northern Rockies, Mary Wulff-Tilford

STAND LOCATIONS

Date of Discovery	Location and Description of Stand	Site Record #

Sage

Salvia spp.   Labiatae

IMPACT LEVEL: 2

OTHER NAMES

Clary, Clear-eye, Black Sage, White Sage, Thistle Sage, Mediterranean Sage, Lanceleaf Sage.

DESCRIPTION

Sages are members of the Mint Family, and like other family members they have four-sided stems and opposite leaves. Most Sages present their flowers in white to blue whorled clusters along the top third of the plant, and most western Sages have (to varying degrees) a characteristic sage-like odor that is very similar to the domestic variety in your spice cabinet *(Salvia officinalis)*. However, don't scout for Sage exclusively by smell... several other plants of entirely different botanical families smell like Sage. One example is Sagebrush *(Artemisia species)*, a member of the Sunflower/Daisy Family.

This genus is too large and diverse to include here... check with your local herbarium and reference books that are specific to your bioregion... or use the garden variety.

HABITAT

Generally speaking, Sages are at home in dry, sunny areas. Many of the lower elevation varieties, such as *S. clevelandii, S. leucophylla,* and *S. apiana* of the Mountain Southwest, and *S. dorrii* of the Great Basin and Northwest, are commonly found blanketing the foothills. Some varieties (such as *S. reflexa*) thrive at elevations as high as 8000', but are generally smaller and are found in far less abundance.

216

Sage

ACTIONS
Antiseptic, astringent, hemostatic, anti-hidrotic, alterative, tonic.

PROPAGATION & GROWTH CHARACTERISTICS
The fashion in which *Saliva species* chooses to reproduce is as diverse as the genus itself. Some Sages grow as annuals, others as biennials or perennials. Most are drought tolerant and prefer soils that are low in organic matter. In addition to culinary varieties, dozens of native Sages are available through nurseries, particularly those which specialize in native plants.

GATHERING SEASON AND GENERAL GUIDELINES
Sage can be gathered anytime, but the strongest herb is gathered from blooming plants. The young, stem-tip shoots are the best tasting part of the plant and are best for use in teas. Pluck the tips, the leaves, or cut the flowering stems.

Some Sages are frowned upon by livestock owners and herbicide enthusiasts. Lanceleaf Sage *(S. reflexa)* is said to contain high levels of nitrates and is reputedly toxic to livestock. Mediterranean Sage *(S. aethiopis)* form tumbleweeds and are viewed by some as troublesome enough to warrant chemical warfare... check before you gather.

Although edible, none of the wild varieties are as palatable as their culinary cousins. In fact, most are so strong (even in small amounts) that they will transform your best recipes into an effective moth repellent.

PARTS USED
All above-ground parts.

CARE AFTER GATHERING
The leaves, stems, and flowers can be used fresh or dried in infusions and poultices.
TINCTURE DRIED HERB: 1:5, 50% alcohol.

Sage

PLANT/ANIMAL INTERDEPENDENCE

Sages are foraged upon by a variety of animals, but it serves a more definitive role as a source of cover and habitat. This holds particularly true where Sage grows in thick abundance, such as many areas in the mountain foothills of Southern California. Beneath these dense herbal canopies lives a biocommunity of rodents, reptiles, ground-dwelling birds, and insects. Many creatures spend their entire lives there... eating, sleeping, reproducing and dying within the protective cover of *Salvia.*

Sage is also a very effective pollinator-attractor. It is popular among bees and beekeepers alike, as nothing compares to the tangy sweetness of Sage honey.

IMPACT CONSIDERATIONS

Salvia is an abundant herb throughout North America and is in no *collective* danger of disappearing. However, many of the Sage-covered canyons and hills we played in as children are now bound with asphalt and stucco, and many of the animals that used to inhabit them are disappearing. Natural abundance is a gift to be appreciated... not taken for granted. The next time you look across an expanse of Sage, please consider what the future may hold.

PHOTO REFERENCES

The Audubon Society Field Guide to North American Wildflowers, Richard Spellenberg

Weeds of the West, The Western Society of Weed Science

TECHNICAL REFERENCES

Medicinal Plants of the Desert and Canyon West, Michael Moore

The Holistic Herbal, David Hoffmann

The Herb Book, John Lust

Quick Reference - Medicinal Plants of the Northern Rockies, Mary Wulff-Tilford

Sage

STAND LOCATIONS

Date of Discovery	Location and Description of Stand	Site Record #

Field Notes

Self Heal

Prunella vulgaris   Labiatae

IMPACT LEVEL: 2

OTHER NAMES
Heal-all, All-heal, Woundwort.

DESCRIPTION
Self Heal is a member of the Mint Family, and like others in the *Labiatae* clan, it has square stems and opposing leaves. But unlike most other mints, Self Heal has no distinguishable odor. It is a small plant, seldom reaching a height over 10". The lance-shaped to broadly ovate leaves have distinct petioles and often have toothed margins (but not always). The stems of Self Heal are weak, and often the lower few inches of the stem will lay flat on top of the ground before curving upward.
Flowers are blue-violet, and grow in whorled, cob-like, ½"-2" clusters at the top of the plant.

HABITAT
Self Heal is at home in moist meadows and pastures, along road margins, and shady wooded areas. It occurs most frequently in areas frequented by livestock.
This plant, although widely distributed across North America, is seldom seen growing in what could be considered profuse stands. Instead, it is usually found in groups of a few here... a few there... perhaps a dozen somewhere else. It is often obscured by taller plants and grasses and commonly goes unnoticed by the unfocused eye.

ACTIONS
Astringent, tonic, vulnerary, anti-inflammatory.

Self Heal

PROPAGATION & GROWTH CHARACTERISTICS
Self Heal is a rhizomatous perennial that can be introduced into the herb garden by the transplanting of root cuttings. The plant needs consistent moisture, rich soil, and at least 50% shade conditions in order to thrive. Although the plant produces viable seed which can also be planted into the garden, the seeds are tiny and are dispersed quickly after reaching maturity.

Self Heal seems to enjoy the fringes of areas that receive constant doses of soil compression. This is probably attributed to the plant's shallow rhizomes, which require a certain degree of soil density in order to support the weak-stemmed upper plant.

GATHERING SEASON AND GENERAL GUIDELINES
Gather this plant while it is blooming. The juiciest, most useful part of the plant is the base of the stem, so cut the plant just above ground level with sharp shears. Take care not to pull the plants when cutting... this may damage the roots and compromise next year's growth. Gather from the margins of the largest stands you can find, and avoid walking between the plants whenever possible. Like many rhizomatous plants, Self Heal often grows in "colonies" that are offshoots from just a few (or even one) roots. If the host roots are damaged, the entire group of plants may die.

Avoid areas that are particularly marshy, and gather during dry weather to prevent excessive soil compression.

PARTS USED
Entire above-ground plant.

CARE AFTER GATHERING
Self Heal is best if used fresh, but can be dried and stored for up to six months for use in tea. It has a pleasant flavor, and is useful in poultice form for soothing sore gums and minor injuries and irritations to the skin. According to herbalist Michael Moore, fresh Self Heal juice can be preserved

Self Heal

by mixing it with twenty-five percent vodka (75% juice, 25% vodka), or with 10% ethanol (grain alcohol). This formula can be stored and used as needed on minor wounds and irritations.

If you want to dry this herb, give it plenty of air circulation or mold will develop.

√ COMMON COMPANION HERBS
Stinging Nettle, Horsetail, False Solomon's Seal, Cow Parsnip, other Mints...

PLANT/ANIMAL INTERDEPENDENCE
Although not a primary source of forage, most herbivores will eat Self Heal. The rhizomes of this plant serve as soil aerators and help allow the introduction of beneficial organisms. The flowers are attractive to pollinators, and help to draw them down into the lower reaches of the forest flora.

√ IMPACT CONSIDERATIONS
When gathering this herb in the presence of livestock, consider the probability of vicarious impact and be aware that herbicides may be present, particularly if plants such as St. John's Wort, Knapweed, or Tansy are nearby. Avoid gathering anywhere near roadways, as this plant collects lead compounds and other toxic substances readily.

PHOTO REFERENCES
Magic and Medicine of Plants, Reader's Digest Books
Northwest Weeds, Ronald J. Taylor
The New Age Herbalist, Richard Mabey (also has technical information)

TECHINICAL REFERENCES
Medicinal Plants of the Mountain West, Michael Moore
The Holistic Herbal, David Hoffmann

Self Heal

Edible and Medicinal Plants of the Rocky Mountains and Neighbouring Territories, Terry Willard, Ph.D.

Quick Reference - Medicinal Plants of the Northern Rockies, Mary Wulff-Tilford

STAND LOCATIONS

Date of Discovery	Location and Description of Stand	Site Record #

Shepherd's Purse

Capsella bursa-pastoris   Cruciferae

IMPACT LEVEL: 1

OTHER NAMES
Bursa, Thlaspi bursa-pastoris

DESCRIPTION
Shepherd's Purse is a common "lawn & vacant lot weed".   Growth begins as a basal rosette of petiolate, 1"-2" leaves that are hairy underneath and smooth above.   The upper plant consists of one or more slender, erect stems that can grow to about 20" tall.

The lanceolate, stalkless leaves of the upper plant grow alternately, clasping the stem at their base.   The lower leaves of the plant are generally deeply lobed, whereas the upper leaves become progressvely fewer and less lobed.

The flowers are small and white and are presented on elongated racemes at the top of the plant. **The flowers develop into seed bearing capsules that look like tiny (½" or less), sharply heart-shaped purses... a characteristic that likely earned the plant its common name.**
These "little purses" are two-celled, have a single ridge along one side; and are slightly concave along the other.   Each "purse-cell" contains *several tiny seeds.*

Many herbalists take the "purse" characteristic of Shepherd's Purse for granted and don't look closely enough when identifying the plant before gathering.   Subsequently, many of them end up gathering and using the wrong plant. Although the misidentified plant is usually another harmless member of the Mustard Family *(Cruciferae)*, it is often a medicinally useless substitute.

Of   the   plants   most   commonly   misidentified   as

Shepherd's Purse

Shepherd's Purse, *Thlaspi arvense* (Field Pennycress) is perhaps on the very top of the list. Like other plants that are mistaken for Shepherd's Purse, Field Pennycress has distinctive differences in its seed capsules (or *pods*). **The seed pods of Pennycress and most other impostors are ovate to nearly circular, not heart-shaped. Like Shepherd's Purse the capsules have two cells, *but each cell only has two seeds.*** Pennycress also has an unpleasant (although not overwhelming) odor about it.

Down on the list of impostors we also have *Thlapsi fendleri* (Wild Candytuft), which has seed pods that more closely resemble those of Shepherd's Purse, but again have only two seeds per capsule cell. The pods are also narrower, and are better described as arrow-shaped, as opposed to heart-shaped. This plant can also be distinguished from Shepherd's Purse by its waxy, toothed leaves, smaller overall size, and mat-like growth characteristic.

And the list goes on...

Lepidium perfoliatum (Clasping Pepperweed) is another *Cruciferae* that is commonly misidentified as Shepherd's Purse, but in this case there is less excuse for error. Clasping Pepperweed has leaves that are entirely different than those of Shepherd's Purse, as they wrap around the stem to give an appearance of little impaled lily pads. This and other Pepperweeds also have circular (*not* heart-shaped) seed pods that contain only two seeds per cell.

HABITAT

Shepherd's Purse is a European import that is widely distributed across North America. It is common in cultivated fields, gardens, lawns, vacant lots, areas subject to livestock, and other disturbed areas. It can be found in just about any environment; from the cracks in city streets to remote mountain campsites. It is adaptable to any elevation, ranging from below sea level to timberline.

Shepherd's Purse

Heart-shaped seed capsules are divided into two parts, each containing several seeds.
Other plants that look like Shepherd's Purse have seed capsules that are divided, but each part contains only two seeds.

Capsella spp.

Shepherd's Purse

ACTIONS
Diuretic, astringent, uterine stimulant.

PROPAGATION & GROWTH CHARACTERISTICS
Shepherd's Purse is an annual that seeds itself very abundantly. It tolerates just about any conditions, but like most of us it prefers rich, well-drained soil and a good combination of sun and moisture.

This plant is very prolific and tends to become a permanent resident if left alone in the garden. It competes well with other "weeds" but generally does not overwhelm them, and is frequently seen growing as part of a natural bouquet of grasses and other plants.

Shepherd's Purse is viewed as "a troublesome weed" by many and is often subjected to eradication efforts. For this reason, I strongly discourage the transport of this herb into areas where it is not yet established.

GATHERING SEASON AND GENERAL GUIDELINES
As long as Shepherd's Purse is green and healthy, the entire plant can be gathered anytime. However, it's wise to wait until after the formation of seed capsules. Otherwise positive identification can be difficult.

PARTS USED
The entire plant, roots and all.

CARE AFTER GATHERING
This plant does not keep well and should be gathered for short term use or for tincturing. To use the herb in tea, dry it on butcher paper and use it shortly thereafter.

FRESH HERB TINCTURE: 1:2 Ratio; DRIED HERB: 1:5 Ratio, in 50% (100 Proof) alcohol.

Fresh Shepherd's Purse is edible and is very nutritious. It has a peppery flavor and is a nice addition to salads and sandwiches when gathered young. The seeds are sometimes dried and used as a pepper substitute.

Shepherd's Purse

COMMON COMPANION HERBS
Absolutely limitless.

PLANT/ANIMAL INTERDEPENDENCE
Most herbivores like the taste of Shepherd's Purse, although it seldom serves as a primary source of forage. The peppery seeds and seed capsules are consumed by an assortment of birds and small rodents.

Like all annual plants, Shepherd's Purse completely donates itself to the soil each and every year... but unlike most plants it adds extra nutrients through a very specialized process. The seed capsules, when wet, become sticky and attractive to ants and other insects. Many of these creatures stick to the capsules, die, and are carried to the soil as food for seedlings and neighboring plants.

IMPACT CONSIDERATIONS
Shepherd's Purse is an abundant, weedy herb that will likely endure humanity longer than humanity can endure itself. For this reason, this plant should be considered for use before other, more environmentally sensitive herbs are employed.

The EcoHerbalist should also remember that Shepherd's Purse is here in North America by human device, and compounded interferences with natural balances (such as weed control) may occur when it is introduced into a pristine environment. Let's leave the distribution of this herbal ally to the *real* experts... our natural animal companions.

PHOTO REFERENCES
Weeds of the West, Western Society of Weed Science (has good photos of *Pennycress* and *Pepperweed* too)
Magic and Medicine of Plants, Reader's Digest Books
The New Age Herbalist, Richard Mabey
Northwest Weeds, Ronald J. Taylor
The Audubon Society Field Guide to North American Wildflowers, Richard Spellenberg

Shepherd's Purse

TECHNICAL REFERENCES
Medicinal Plants of the Canyon and Desert West, Michael Moore

Wise Woman Herbal for the Childbearing Year, Susun S. Weed

The Holistic Herbal, David Hoffmann

Discovering Wild Plants, Janice J. Schofield (also has good photo)

Edible and Medicinal Plants of the Rocky Mountains and Neighbouring Territories, Terry Willard, Ph.D.

Quick Reference - Medicinal Plants of the Northern Rockies, Mary Wulff-Tilford

STAND LOCATIONS

Date of Discovery	Location and Description of Stand	Site Record #

Stinging Nettle

Urtica dioica   Urticaceae

IMPACT LEVEL: 2

OTHER NAMES
Nettle, Common Nettle.

DESCRIPTION
If you haven't discovered this plant, then odds are it hasn't discovered *you* either. Most people never forget the introductory sting of their first encounter with Stinging Nettle and have a vivid image of the plant burned into memory as a standby defense mechanism. *Urtica dioica* introduced itself to me when I was about 12 years old, and identification of the plant has been easy for me ever since. For those of you who have not yet encountered this old and trusted (if not overt) ally and wish to initiate an introduction on *your* terms, a general description follows.

Stinging Nettle grows on strong, erect stems that can reach up to 6' in height. The plant's fibrous stems are square, much like many members of the unrelated Mint Family.

The lanceolate, sharply toothed, opposite leaves range from 1"-6" in length and also look like Mint. However, *unlike* Mint, the undersides of the leaves are covered with tiny, hollow hairs that contain a combination of formic acid and antigenic protein. When the plant is touched these constituents are *injected* into the skin under pressure, in a manner not unlike tiny hypodermic needles.

Flowers are rather unimpressive; appearing as compact, drooping clusters of tiny greenish blossoms beneath the base of the upper leaves.

Stinging Nettle

Urtica species

The stems contain linear fibers that are very, *very*

Stinging Nettle

strong. These fibers provide an excellent source of cordage and have been used for thousands of years in the production of rope and clothing fabric. Nettle fiber is still available today (particularly in Europe and Asia), and is generally quite expensive.

HABITAT
Moist riparian areas and meadows. Stinging Nettle is widespread across North America at elevations ranging from 2000' to 9000'.

ACTIONS
Nutritive, astringent, diuretic, tonic.

PROPAGATION & GROWTH CHARACTERISTICS
Stinging Nettle is a perennial that reproduces largely off of its network of weak rhizomes, and to a lesser degree by seed. Although it is frequently found in abundance, it tends to be specific and finicky about where it chooses to live. One can often find a thick, healthy stand of several hundred plants within a 50' strip of streambank, and not a single other within the rest of the drainage.

Although I have had some success with the transplant of root cuttings, most of my efforts (and the efforts of others) have ended in failure. This could very well be due to the fragility of the roots... they are small and are very easily damaged.. If you insist upon transplanting root cuttings, gather far more than seems necessary (a foot or more) off of each rhizome, bearing in mind that you are killing the parent plant. Plant the cutting in a medium and habitat that replicates the point of origin as closely as possible, then keep the transplant evenly moist throughout its growth.

GATHERING SEASON AND GENERAL GUIDELINES
Gather Nettles before the plants begin to bloom in early spring. If you are gathering Nettles to eat (they are delicious boiled and served with lemon and butter), get them as

Stinging Nettle

early as they can be positively identified. The young plants often appear rust or maroon-colored until they are 6" high or so, and is the stage at which the plants are most palatable. They will turn green as they cook, *and should always be cooked very thoroughly.* Cooking neutralizes the formic acid, rendering the plant safe to eat. Older plants tend to be bitter as a potherb, but are still useful for tea *if* they have not bloomed.

This herb should not be used after it has begun its bloom cycle, as the older leaves develop *cystoliths*, gritty particles that can be irritating to the kidneys.

Wear gloves and a long-sleeved shirt when gathering this herb. Cut the stems well above ground level, taking care not to disturb the roots. For easy handling, put the cuttings top-down in a paper shopping bag. If you experience a sting during your gathering, try squeezing some of the juice from a cut stem of the same plant and applying it to the affected area... surprisingly, this will often provide immediate relief. If relief does not occur, don't fret. The sting is short-lived, and the pain should subside in an hour or so. A poultice of *Plantain* or *Penstemon* may also be useful.

PARTS USED
The whole upper plant.

CARE AFTER GATHERING
The dried herb is most often used as an infusion. We use the crushed and dried leaves as a nutritional food garnish as well. It is very good for you, as it contains a wide spectrum of essential vitamins and minerals in quantities that can be readily assimilated by the body.

To dry Stinging Nettle, spread the fresh plants loosely atop butcher paper or a non-metallic screen. Allow for plenty of dry air circulation and rearrange the herb frequently to prevent development of mold. **Do not wash this herb before drying it or spoilage will almost certainly occur.**

Store the herb in an airtight container *after it has*

Stinging Nettle

dried completely. The leaves and stems should be brittle and crumbly. If the stems are at all rubbery, then the drying process is incomplete. The dried herb will keep for up to a year, and can be used for tea by steeping in near-boiling water. Use a quantity to suit your taste.

COMMON COMPANION HERBS

Angelica, Cow Parsnip, Horsetail, Mints, Cleavers, Sweetroot, Pyrola...

PLANT/ANIMAL INTERDEPENDENCE

Stinging Nettle serves well-defined purposes as a source of shelter and food for its companions. Thick stands of this plant are almost always inhabited by various reptiles, amphibians, ground-dwelling birds and rodents that take advantage of the plant's painfully protective cover. In fact, this plant protects delicate riparian habitats by discouraging human encroachment... a feat that indeed deserves applause.

Stinging Nettle decomposes rapidly and completely, contributing substantial quantities of nitrogen and mineral nutrients into the soil.

IMPACT CONSIDERATIONS

The soil in which this plant lives is often soft and easily compacted. This means that the delicate, generally shallow roots of the plants may be vulnerable to the effects of human feet. Also be aware of the likely presence of animals and their dwellings, particularly in the denser stands. Keep your harvest at the outer edges of the stand and gather very conservatively. Visual impact upon a stand directly equates to the quality of the habitat it provides... if you can see the results of your harvest, then you have taken too much. Keep accurate records of your observations during each visit to a site, and be especially sensitive to the impact your presence alone may have upon the inhabitants of a stand. If you find that creatures are vacating despite conservative gathering efforts, it is obvious that your presence has disrupted the

Stinging Nettle

biocommunity in and around the stand.

PHOTO REFERENCES

Northwest Weeds, Ronald J. Taylor

Nature Bound Pocket Field Guide, Ron Dawson

Edible and Medicinal Plants of the Rocky Mountains and Neighbouring Territories, Terry Willard Ph.D. (also has technical information)

Discovering Wild Plants, Janice J. Schofield (also has technical information)

Weeds of the West, Western Society of Weed Science

The New Age Herbalist, Richard Mabey (also has technical information)

TECHNICAL REFERENCES

Medicinal Plants of the Mountain West, Michael Moore

Healing Wise, Susun S. Weed

The Holistic Herbal, David Hoffmann

The Male Herbal, James Green

The Herb Book, John Lust

The Healing Herbs, Michael Castleman

Quick Reference - Medicinal Plants of the Northern Rockies, Mary Wulff-Tilford

Stinging Nettle

STAND LOCATIONS

Date of Discovery	Location and Description of Stand	Site Record #

Field Notes

St. John's Wort

Hypericum spp   Hypericaceae

IMPACT LEVEL: 1

OTHER NAMES
Western St. John's Wort, Bog St. John's Wort, Canada St. John's Wort, Goatweed, Klamath Weed.

DESCRIPTION
At least four varieties of *Hypericum* can be found in the Western United States and Canada, with *H. formosum* and *H. perforatum* the most common and widespread.

St. John's Wort is a perennial with many-branched stems and ovate to lanceolate leaves that are undivided, opposite, and stalkless. The leaves have tiny purplish-black dots. These little dots contain the active ingredient *hypericin.* When rubbed between the fingertips, this constituent will sometimes stain your skin red.

The yellow, 3/4", 5-petalled flowers are presented in multiple inflorescences along the top third of the 12"-36" tall plants *(H. perforatum* and *H. formosum...* other species are smaller) and also have tiny purplish-black dots on the petals, particularly at the margins. However, *H. majus* does not have any black dots at all.

St. John's Wort is viewed as a very troublesome weed by many, and where it is present it is likely to be well known among local agriculturalists. Check with your Extension Agent for the species in your bioregion.

HABITAT
H. perforatum (Goatweed or Klamath Weed) is common to dry, sunny subalpine hillsides. It ranges from the Pacific Coast to the Rocky Mountain States; Colorado to Montana. *H. formosum* (Western St. John's Wort) prefers moister areas,

St. John's Wort

and is frequently found on north-facing hillsides at the higher, subalpine elevations (5000' - 8000').
H. anagalloides (Bog St. John's Wort) is especially common to moist, subalpine areas of the Sierras, and is sporadically distributed throughout the Interior Mountain West from Mexico into British Columbia..
H. majus (Canada St. John's Wort) is the least common of all four. It is rare to the Western U.S., and occurs sporadically across the Eastern third of North America.

ACTIONS
Astringent, anti-inflammatory, vulnerary, sedative.

PROPAGATION & GROWTH CHARACTERISTICS
St. John's Wort is a perennial that reproduces from short runners or by seed. In areas where this plant is found, it is generally found in abundance. Some varieties of St. John's Wort, such as *Hypericum perforatum* were introduced from Europe, and remain in the same areas where they were first introduced through livestock grazing decades ago. It seems that wherever this plant has established itself it has become a stubborn and persistent resident.
St. John's Wort reproduces freely and vigorously. It ruthlessly competes with native plants and should not be introduced into pristine areas under any circumstances. I also strongly discourage introduction of this plant into the herb garden. The seeds are *very* small and are quickly distributed by birds, rainfall, passerby, wind, etc.. Eventually they may find their way out of the garden and into the surrounding area, sparking a potentially lethal chain reaction of vicarious impact within the ecosystem.
Although this is a very useful plant ally to the herbalist, care must be taken not to encourage its proliferation in areas where it has not yet established itself. To do so would almost certainly guarantee herbicidal intervention sometime in the future.

St. John's Wort

GATHERING SEASON AND GENERAL GUIDELINES
St. John's Wort should be gathered when it is beginning to bloom (late June to August). Using a sharp pair of pruning shears, clip the top 6–12" off mature plants (the ones that are largest and are multi-branched).

Always wear gloves when gathering this herb, as some people experience a photo–sensitive reaction after reaching maximum skin absorption of the constituent hypericin. If you experience an *acute* reaction, it stands to reason that you should not use this herb.

PARTS USED
Although the herb industry has sensationalized the exclusive use of St John's Wort flowers, the entire plant contains active constituents and can be used. The collection of upper stems, leaves, and flowers eliminates hour upon hour of needless and meticulous plucking and causes very little harm to this impact resilient perennial.

CARE AFTER GATHERING
St. John's Wort makes a wonderful oil infusion that is as beautiful as it is useful. The finished product is a clear, ruby red... like claret wine, and is an excellent addition to salves and ointments. It is also good just as an oil; for topical application. To make oil wilt the herb first, then chop the flowers, stems, and leaves as finely as possible (we use a food processor) and put it into a large glass jar. Cover the herb with enough olive oil to put a ½", clear film over it. Cover the jar tightly and allow the herb to infuse for at least one month before straining through a jelly bag or clean cloth. Store the oil in an airtight jar.

The herb can be tinctured as well. TINCTURE FRESH STEMS, LEAVES, AND FLOWERS: 1:2 Ratio, 50% alcohol.

COMMON COMPANION HERBS
Mullein, Fireweed, Arnica, Balsamroot, Shepherd's Purse, Oregon Grape...

St. John's Wort

PLANT/ANIMAL INTERDEPENDENCE
St. John's Wort is reputedly toxic to livestock, causing photosensitivity that results in skin irritations (it sometimes does this to humans too). Although it is not frequently foraged, larger stands do provide cover and habitat for rodents and the sleeping deer. The flowers are very attractive to bees and other pollinators.

IMPACT CONSIDERATIONS
Always beware of herbicidal maniacs when you gather this plant, and take extra care not to carry the seeds away from established stands.

In recent years an insect has been introduced into populations of St. John's Wort to provide "biological control" of this "noxious weed". Whether or not this voracious little bug is eating *only* St. John's Wort remains to be seen, but I personally doubt it. Shake off your herb well before transporting, or better yet... tincture it in the field.

PHOTO REFERENCES
Weeds of the West, The Western Society of Weed Science
Northwest Weeds, Ronald J. Taylor
Magic and Medicine of Plants, Reader's Digest Books
The New Age Herbalist, Richard Mabey (also has technical information)

TECHNICAL REFERENCES
Medicinal Plants of the Pacific West, Michael Moore
Wise Woman Ways - Menopausal Years, Susun S. Weed
The Holistic Herbal, David Hoffmann
Quick Reference - Medicinal Plants of the Northern Rockies, Mary Wulff-Tilford
Out of the Earth, Simon Y. Mills

St. John's Wort

STAND LOCATIONS

Date of Discovery	Location and Description of Stand	Site Record #

Field Notes

Uva-Ursi

Arctostaphylos uva-ursi   Ericaceae

IMPACT LEVEL: 2

OTHER NAMES
Bearberry, Kinnikinnick, Red Bear's Grape, Tinnick, Mealberry, Chipmunk's Apples.

DESCRIPTION
Uva-ursi is a low-growing shrub that is often seen covering the forest floor in dense mats. The plant has long, woody, reddish-brown runners that put down roots from intermittent nodes.

The alternate leaves are ¼" to 3/4" long, ovate to lance-shaped, dark green and leathery in texture.

Arctostaphylos uva-ursi

Uva-ursi

Flowers are small (½" or less), pink, and urn-shaped. The flowers present themselves in terminal clusters of 1-4 per plant, and later develop into bright red, ¼" berries that look like tiny apples. The berries have a mealy, yellow inner pith and a proportionately large seed.

HABITAT

Uva-ursi is common to coniferous forests throughout most western forests of North America, with the exception of Central and Southern California, where it does not occur at all. However, it does have an equally useful relative in that region... *Arctostaphylos manzanita* (Common Manzanita), a large (up to 20') evergreen shrub that is common from the Northern Sierra foothills to the mountains of Southern California. Aside from being a much larger shrub, Manzanita has leaves, flowers, and berries that are very similar to Uva-ursi.

Uva-ursi prefers sunny, dry forest clearings, and is common at elevations ranging from 2500' to timberline.

ACTIONS

Uva-ursi contains *alot* of tannins, and is therefore a very strong astringent. Internally, it is useful for acute urinary tract infections, **but can become irritating to the kidneys and bladder if used for more than 24-48 hours.**

It should not be used internally during pregnancy.

Topically it is useful as a protective first aid dressing, or in a *sitz bath*, for the reduction of swollen hemorrhoidal tissues.

PROPAGATION & GROWTH CHARACTERISTICS

Uva-ursi is a hardy perennial that can be established from transplants, root cuttings, or by seed.

Seeds must be cold-stratified in order to germinate. Collect the berries as late in the fall as possible, then freeze them prior to planting in the spring. Or direct-seed during the fall.

243

Uva-ursi

Root cuttings can be started indoors, in a medium of peat moss and perlite. Keep the cuttings evenly moist until sprouting occurs. This plant will only establish itself in an environment that accurately fits its habitat needs. Don't try planting Uva-ursi into your rock garden if you live in Palm Springs... it won't work! Some nurseries that specialize in native ground covers sell established plants. Manzanita is also available (although it grows *very slowly*).

Arctostaphylos is very cold hardy, and is often found in a healthy, green condition beneath a thick blanket of snow.

GATHERING SEASON AND GENRAL GUIDELINES

Uva-ursi can be gathered anytime that the plant is in good condition. To gather it, find a large stand and carefully clip a foot or less from *loose* runners. If you meet resistance when pulling a runner toward you, **stop,** the stem has taken root. Whenever possible, gather from plants that are hanging over a boulder or a steep bank. This will alllow you to clip long, free-hanging stems without impacting the root system or the soil surrounding the parent plants.

Although this plant appears as though it would be resilient to harvest impact, Mary and I have found that it is not. Some of the stands that we took great care in moving through and gathering from have shown significant die-back over a two year period of observation. For this reason, *gather very conservatively from the periphery of the stand.* Gather from multiple sites, and monitor the long-term effects of your gathering.

PARTS USED

Leaves, stems, flowers and berries.

CARE AFTER GATHERING

The leathery nature of this plant's leaf and stem structure makes it rather insoluble in water. For use in infusions, the herb should be dried first to break down the

244

Uva-ursi

herb's surface structures. If you plan on using it fresh, you can "pickle" it and make it more soluble. This is accomplished by wetting the leaves with a small amount of hard booze (brandy, vodka, etc.) and allowing it to sit for an hour or so before simmering it for twenty minutes (decoction). The alcohol acts as a solvent, breaking down the plant tissues and making the constituents more accessible.

TO TINCTURE THE FRESH HERB: 1:5 Ratio, 50% (100 Proof) alcohol.

COMMON COMPANION HERBS

Arnica, Valerian, Yarrow, Balsamroot, Penstemon, Mullein, Oregon Grape...

PLANT/ANIMAL INTERDEPENDENCE

Arctostaphylos and *Uva-ursi* essentially translates to "bear grapes" in english. The plant earned its name through the gastronomic love of bears.

The berries are relished by other animals as well, and the leaves are a very important source of mid-winter forage. Throughout the winter, deer, elk, grouse and squirrels dig through the snow in search of Uva-ursi berries and to some degree, the evergreen foliage. Without such hardy evergreens, these animals could face grave circumstances.

The creeping, root-bound nature of this plant makes it an effective soil retention agent, particularly where it is growing on hillsides or at the edge of a steep bank.

IMPACT CONSIDERATIONS

The abundance and widespread range of this plant offers little excuse for over-harvesting a single stand. Reduce your impact by gathering conservatively from several different sites. Avoid walking on the plants, and never gather when the soil is wet and vulnerable to human feet.

Stay alert for any signs of forage activity. The berries are often passed through the digestive tracts of animals in recognizable form. If active foraging is evident, move onward

Uva-ursi

to another stand, or choose an alternative such as *Alumroot, Pyrola,* or *Goldenrod.*

In recent years, Uva-ursi and Manzanita have gained some popularity in the floral industry. The evergreen plants stand well in bouquets and make attractive fillers. Although Manzanita is protected by California state law, I have seen evidence (and actually witnessed the act) of illegal, commercial-scale harvest of this beautiful and slow-growing shrub.

Watch the stands of these plants in your bioregion. If plants start disappearing, check with your local floral wholesaler.

PHOTO REFERENCES

The Audubon Society Field Guide to North American Wildflowers, Richard Spellenberg (photos of *A. uva-ursi)*

The Audubon Society Field Guide to North American Trees - Western Region, Elbert L. Little (photo of *A. manzanita)*

Nature Bound Pocket Field Guide, Ron Dawson (Kinnickinnick)

Magic and Medicine of Plants, Reader's Digest Books (Bearberry)

TECHNICAL REFERENCES

Medicinal Plants of the Pacific West, Michael Moore

Wise Woman Herbal for the Childbearing Year, Susun S. Weed

Discovering Wild Plants, Janice J. Schofield (also has photos)

The Holistic Herbal, David Hoffmann ("Bearberry")

The Herb Book, John Lust ("Bearberry")

Edible and Medicinal Plants of the Rocky Mountains and Neighbouring Territories, Terry Willard, Ph.D. ("Bearberry" - also has photos)

Quick Reference - Medicinal Plants of the Northern Rockies, Mary Wulff-Tilford

Uva-ursi

STAND LOCATIONS

Date of Discovery	Location and Description of Stand	Site Record #

Field Notes

Valerian

Valeriana spp.   Valerianaceae

IMPACT LEVEL: 2

OTHER NAMES
Mountain Valerian, Sitka Valerian, "Tobacco Root", Edible Valerian.

DESCRIPTION
Valerian is easy to identify by its **strongly aromatic roots, which some people relate to the odor of dirty socks.** I think that the odor of Valerian root is pleasantly "Earthy". Perhaps I've been atop the mountain too long... or maybe I need to change my socks! Anyway...

The simple (undivided) and lanceolate basal leaves appear in clusters and are usually larger than the upper leaves. The upper leaves are opposite and pinnately divided into lance-shaped leaflets that are progressively smaller toward the top of the plant.

Flowers range from white to pink, and are borne in branched, terminate clusters. The individual flowers are small and have three stamens.

Roots are fibrous, stringy, brown, *and pungent.*

HABITAT
Most Valerians are found in moist subalpine meadows and montaine forests, up to timberline. They are frequently seen growing from moist, north-facing roadbanks and steep hillsides.

Valeriana species is widespread and varied throughout the Mountain West, from British Columbia to Mexico.

Valerian

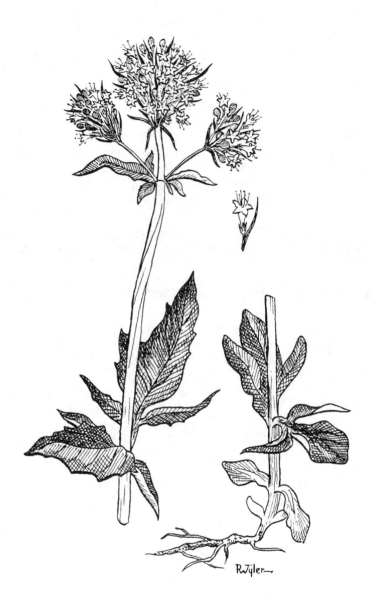

Valeriana species

Valerian

ACTIONS
Sedative, antispasmodic, carminative, hypotensive.

PROPAGATION & GROWTH CHARACTERISTICS
Valerian is a perennial that can be started from seed or from young transplants. It likes rich soil that contains at least moderate amounts of organic matter and plenty of water, although it will survive drought conditions. It tolerates a wide range of soil pH levels, and prefers partial shade to full sun.

Seed collection is often difficult, as the plant dies back quickly after blooming. Mature plants do not transplant well, but seedlings do.

Valerian is easy to establish in the herb garden and should be. It is available through several seed companies and nurseries.

GATHERING SEASON AND GENERAL GUIDELINES
Gather Valerian in the fall, this is when the roots are strongest. Since this plant dies back shortly after blooming, locating the fall plants is often difficult. For this reason, it's a good idea to choose the plants you want earlier in the summer. Mark the locations of the plants with sticks or rocks, and take accurate notes of any landmarks (such as tree stumps, large rocks, etc.). When you return in the fall to dig the roots, you will still be able to locate them. If the aerial parts have completely died back, the plant is still easy to identify by its distinctive odor (familiarize yourself with the earthy pungency beforehand).

Gather this plant conservatively from healthy stands. As always, avoid gathering when the ground is wet and prone to soil compaction.

If seeds are still on the plant when you gather, scatter them around the plant and bury a few directly into the hole you create.

PARTS USED
Primarily the root, but the entire plant is useful.

Valerian

CARE AFTER GATHERING ✳

This herb can be used in fresh or dried form. The roots actually become more pungent after they are dried, and will keep for a year or more if properly stored. Use either form in tea, or tincture it.

Dry the roots and upper parts by simply spreading it loosely atop butcher paper or a non-metallic screen.

FRESH HERB TINCTURE: 1:2 Ratio; DRIED HERB: 1:5 Ratio, in 50-70% alcohol.

Long term use can lead to depression and mild lethargy.

COMMON COMPANION HERBS

Oregon Grape, Redroot, Uva-ursi, Arnica, Yarrow, Bee Balm, False Solomon's Seal, Clematis...

PLANT/ANIMAL INTERDEPENDENCE

Valerian is browsed upon by deer, elk, bears, moose, and an endless assortment of smaller animals. The household cat may find pleasure in this plant's mildly sedative effect, and there is no reason to deny the probability that wild animals utilize Valerian's soothing effects as well.

IMPACT CONSIDERATIONS

Always look for signs of recent forage before gathering this plant. If signs are evident, choose another stand of plants... this is an abundant herb and there is no reason to deny its availability to our animal friends.

Since the gathering of this perennial root herb entails killing the plant, timing your harvest after the plant has gone to seed is critically important. Close monitoring of your impact is absolutely essential as well.

PHOTO REFERENCES

The New Age Herbalist, Richard Mabey

Edible and Medicinal Plants of the Rocky Mountains and Neighbouring Territorties, Terry Willard, Ph.D. (also contains

Valerian

technical information)

TECHNICAL REFERENCES
Out of the Earth, Simon Y. Mills
Discovering Wild Plants, Janice J. Schofield (also contains good photos)
The Healing Herbs, Michael Castleman
Medicinal Plants of the Pacific West, Michael Moore
Herbal Healing for Women, Rosemary Gladstar
The Holistic Herbal, David Hoffmann
An Elder's Herbal, David Hoffmann
The Male Herbal, James Green
Menopausal Years, Susun S. Weed

STAND LOCATIONS

Date of Discovery	Location and Description of Stand	Site Record #

Wild Ginger

Asarum caudatum   Aristolochiaceae

IMPACT LEVEL: 3

OTHER NAMES
Long-tailed Wild Ginger, Hartwig's Wild Ginger, Lemmon's Wild Ginger.

DESCRIPTION
Wild Ginger is not related to the Ginger found in the supermarket, but it shares some delightful characteristics with it. It is a uniquely pretty inhabitant of dark, coniferous forests in the Mountain Northwest.

A ground-hugging plant with rhizomes that creep through the spongy compost of the forest floor, Wild Ginger emerges in colonies of **dark green, broadly heart-shaped leaves that range in size from about 1"-4" across.** The leaves grow on individual leaf stems that extend directly from the rhizomes.

Flowers are well described as *weird.* **They are purplish-brown to yellowish or greenish in color and grow in pairs. Each flower has a bowl-shaped base and three petal-like lobes, each ½"-3" in length, that taper out from the flower like insect feelers.**

Wild Ginger is sometimes confused with *Pyrola*, which shares a similar growth characteristic and the same habitat. The leaves of *Pyrola* are rounder and less heart-shaped, as well as generally smaller. When the two plants are compared side-by-side the difference becomes obvious.

Perhaps the most distinguishing and delightful characteristic about Wild Ginger is its odor. It smells like

Wild Ginger

store-bought Ginger and is quite pungent, particularly when the leaves are bruised.

Two other species of Wild Ginger are found in the Western United States, *Asarum hartwegii*, which is found in Southern Oregon, Northern California and the Sierras, and *Asarum lemmonii*, also found in the Sierras. Both share similar characteristics with *A. caudatum* and are equally useful.

HABITAT

Moist, shaded woods, particularly in old-growth stands of conifers from 2500'-6000'. The range of this plant extends from the coastal mountains to the west slope of the Rockies in Eastern Idaho.

ACTIONS

Wild Ginger is a secretory stimulant and peripheral vasodilator that helps to improve venous return at skin level. Like its culinary counterpart, Wild Ginger is effective for relief of indigestion.

PROPAGATION AND GROWTH CHARACTERISTICS

Wild Ginger is a perennial that needs lots of shade and consistently moist, acidic soil that is rich in forest compost.

It may be started from fresh seed or carefully handled rhizome cuttings. To minimize impact, I recommend the seed option. Collect the reddish-purple berries as late in the season as possible and plant them in wet peat moss. Transplant while the seedlings are very young to avoid root damage.

Wild Ginger is often found growing in dense patches that predominate the forest floor. The rhizomes are usually very extensive, and what may appear as several individual plants could be the offshoots of a single rhizome. These rhizomes require a considerable accumulation of forest debris in order to survive, and the plant does not tolerate sunshine.

Wild Ginger

GATHERING SEASON AND GENERAL GUIDELINES
Gather Wild Ginger anytime after seeds have fallen in late summer. Avoid periods following precipitation; when the forest floor tends to loose its resiliency. Gather from the periphery of healthy stands, taking care not to compress the soil and compost above the plant's horizontal root system.
Clip the entire upper plant off with sharp pruning shears, just above ground level.
Visual impact is indicative of over-harvest.

PARTS USED
The entire plant is useful in teas and in tincture. Unlike culinary (store bought) Ginger, I have found that the leaves of Wild Ginger are more flavorful than the root. The fresh or freshly dried leaves are excellent for seasoning stir-fry dishes or in marinades.
If you intend to use the root, please be kind to the plant and take only the top inch or so, leaving the rest for perennial regrowth.

CARE AFTER GATHERING
Like most herbs that are gathered from a shady, damp environment, Wild Ginger molds quickly if not dried loosely and with good ventilation. Spread it out on butcher paper or a non-metallic screen and dry it in an airy place that is away from sunlight.
For tincture, fresh is best. FRESH PLANT TINCTURE: 1:2 Ratio; 50% alcohol. DRIED ROOT & LEAVES: 1:5 Ratio; 60% alcohol.
The dried roots and leaves will loose much of their pungency and usefulness after about three months of proper storage, so take only what you need for the immediate future.

COMMON COMPANION HERBS
Coptis, False Solomon's Seal, Huckleberry, Pyrola, Pipsissewa...

Wild Ginger

PLANT/ANIMAL INTERDEPENDENCE

Wild Ginger's extensive, horizontal root system provides an integral life-support structure for the subterranean microcosm. In Wild Ginger's neighborhood the thick, acidic forest floor debris and assortment of mosses composts very slowly and becomes compressed by its own weight. This thick mat can become totally impervious to water, microorganisms, warmth, and even air. To compound this, the absence of sunlight (commonly the case in old-growth forests) allows for very little photosynthesis. The sum of these conditions amounts to a specially adapted assortment of flora, or an environment that is totally void of forest floor plant life. Wild Ginger is a specially adapted plant that serves a critical purpose in this environment, and in many cases it is the key element that stands between life and sterility within delicate forest floor biocommunities.

In what remains of the old-growth forests of the Oregon Cascades, Wild Ginger is often found standing alone beneath the towering firs and cedars. The creeping rhizomes of this plant serve to aerate the forest floor, giving insects, small rodents, and soil-building microorganisms a lease on life. The extensive roots interrupt the continuity of the otherwise impervious mat of debris, allowing the introduction of rainwater and snowmelt. Where sunlight filters through the trees, other plants can flourish, providing sources of nourishing forage that otherwise could not exist. Take away a single element, such as the Wild Ginger, and an entire biocommunity could be compromised.

Nothing is simple, and all is critical in such delicate, special biocommunities. Old-growth forests and plants like Wild Ginger require each other to survive.

IMPACT CONSIDERATIONS

The reason I have rated Wild Ginger a "3" on the Impact Level scale should be obvious to you by now.

When you visit this plant, please take some extra time to look around. Meet the Elders, their children... and listen to

Wild Ginger

what they have to say. Although Wild Ginger is still abundant, its habitat is not. In what remains of North America's old-growth forests, pristine beauty often gives way to trampled campsites and clearcuts just across the creek. Please don't gather any Wild Ginger until you see what lies on the other side.

If you do gather this herb, please make yourself especially aware of its delicate and extremely vulnerable habitat. Always wear soft shoes or none at all in Wild Ginger's house, and gather only during dry weather. *Watch the stands very closely...*

PHOTO REFERENCES

Forest Wildflowers, Dr. Dee Strickler

The Audubon Society Field Guide to North American Wildflowers, Richard Spellenberg

Peterson Field Guides, Eastern/Central Medicinal Plants, Foster & Duke

TECHNICAL REFERENCES

Medicinal Plants of the Pacific West, Michael Moore

Herbal Materia Medica, Michael Moore

STAND LOCATIONS

Date of Discovery	Location and Description of Stand	Site Record #

Wild Rose

Rosa spp.   Rosaceae

IMPACT LEVEL: 2

DESCRIPTION
There is no secret about the identification of *Rosa species*... Wild Roses look like domestic varieties, except they have smaller flowers and leaves.

The leaves are alternate and pinnately divided into 3-11, ½"-1", elliptical to egg-shaped leaflets.

Flowers are pink to red, generally on the smaller side of 2½", have 5 petals and yellow stamens. Like domestic varieties, Wild Roses produce seed-bearing fruits (hips). The hips turn progressively redder after the petals are gone, throughout the fall months.

HABITAT
Wild Roses can be found just about anywhere; up to about 7000' in elevation. *Rosa woodsii*, a variety which is very common to open hillsides and valley floors throughout most of the west, is often found growing in dense thickets that are often frowned upon by farmers, ranchers, and garden enthusiasts.

ACTIONS
Mild laxative, nutrient, diuretic, astringent.

PROPAGATION & GROWTH CHARACTERISTICS
Wild Roses are perennial shrubs that reproduce easily from their roots and seeds. Members of the *Rosa* gang hybridize with one another readily, and will not hesitate to seduce open-pollinating domestic varieties. Wild Roses can be easily started in the garden from stratified seed or the

258

Wild Rose

transplant of rootstock, the latter of which is sold by some nurseries. Just remember... these are "thorny wild things" that may take on a special liking for other *Rosaceaes* in your garden.
      Give the young plants full sun and plenty of water until they are well established.

Rosa species

Wild Rose

GATHERING SEASON AND GENERAL GUIDELINES
Gather the hips after the petals have fallen and they have turned bright red. The tastiest and strongest hips are slightly shriveled and have been through at least one fall frost. The hips often remain in good condition on the bush well into winter but tend to mold easier as they shrivel, so don't wait too long.

The fresh hips make excellent jellies and wine, and are quite tasty eaten fresh... despite the hard seeds.

PARTS USED
The hips.

CARE AFTER GATHERING
Dry the hips on butcher paper or a non-metallic screen and stir them frequently to prevent the development of mold. *Be certain that the hips are completely dry before storing them in an airtight container.* The hips will keep in quality condition for about a year.

To make an infusion (tea), crush some of the dried hips and steep in very hot water. Adjust the quantity of hips to your taste.

COMMON COMPANION HERBS
The possibilities are limitless...

PLANT/ANIMAL INTERDEPENDENCE
Rose hips are relished by birds, deer, coyotes, bears, and just about anyone else who discovers their chewy sweetness. My German Shepherd, *"Willow"* even browses on them when given the opportunity.

Thick, entangled, thorny stands of Wild Roses provide protective cover and habitat for a wide variety of insects and animals.

Bees and other pollinators love the bright and fragrant flowers.

Wild Rose

IMPACT CONSIDERATIONS
Always be aware of the possibility of inhabitants when you gather from stands of Wild Rose, and leave plenty of fruit for dependent wildlife.

This valuable food and medicine plant is often cursed by cattle ranchers, farmers, and garden enthusiasts because of its free-spirited and thorny nature. Check for the presence of herbicides before you begin your harvest. Although a common inhabitant of roadsides and train track easements, these areas are off limits due to toxic residues.

PHOTO REFERENCES
Discovering Wild Plants, Janice J. Schofield (also contains technical information)

The Audubon Society Field Guide to North American Wild Flowers, Richard Spellenberg

Peterson Field Guides - Eastern/Central Medicinal Plants, Foster & Duke

TECHNICAL REFERENCES
Wise Woman Ways - Menopausal Years, Susun S. Weed

The Holistic Herbal, David Hoffmann

Medicinal Plants of the Mountain West, Michael Moore

Natural Healing with Herbs, Humbart Santillo BS, MH

The New Age Herbalist, Richard Mabey (also has good photos)

STAND LOCATIONS

Date of Discovery	Location and Description of Stand	Site Record #

Wild Strawberry

Fragaria spp.   Rosaceae

IMPACT LEVEL: 2

OTHER NAMES
Woods Strawberry, Virginia Strawberry, Blueleaf Strawberry.

DESCRIPTION
Very little is required here... Wild Strawberries look like miniaturized versions of the garden varieties.

Leaves are typically egg-shaped to elliptical and are coarsely toothed, generally growing in divisions of three leaflets. Flowers are white and have five petals. The fruits are much smaller (¼-½") but essentially the same as the ones found in the supermarket.

HABITAT
Several species of Wild Strawberry are common throughout North America. Look for them in forest clearings where the soil is well-drained and rich in organic matter; from about 2000' to about 7500'.

ACTIONS
Mild astringent, mild diuretic, tonic. This is a very safe and gentle herb.

PROPAGATION & GROWTH CHARACTERISTICS
Most species of Wild Strawberry are perennials that get around by runners. These runners can grow to several feet, putting down roots from nodes at various intervals. The young offshoots waste little time sending out runners of their own, and a colony is born. Wild Strawberries will also

Wild Strawberry

reproduce by seed, and use this method as a means of spreading beyond the range of their runners. The seeds, like domestic varieties, are very small and can be passed through the digestive tracts of birds and other small animals in a viable condition.

Wild Strawberries transplant easily and can be introduced into the herb garden anytime that the ground is workable. The plants require ample moisture and sunlight, and thrive in humus-rich soils. They particularly like potassium (potash), which can be provided by working moderate amounts of wood ash into the top soil.

Wild Strawberries can cross-pollinate with non-hybrid garden varieties. This usually results in a strain that yields little or no fruit. So if jam is your intent and you already have a patch of big, juicy berries, you might bear this in mind if your plants are open-pollinated.

GATHERING SEASON AND GENERAL GUIDELINES

Strawberry leaves should be gathered before the plants are in bloom. After blooming begins, the plant's energies are directed toward producing berries and the leaves lose some of their medicinal qualities. Older leaves can be used if they are in good (green) condition, but they simply are not as good.

The fruits (provided you can get to them ahead of our animal and insect companions) are delicious but very small. Although I love to eat them, I usually leave them for those who really need them... our animal companions.

Gather the leaves by pinching a few from several plants. Watch your feet and try to avoid crushing the runners. If by chance you accidentally pull up a plant, simply stick it back into the Earth and tamp the soil down. Chances are it will be fine.

PARTS USED

Primarily the leaves, but the stems are good too.

Wild Strawberry

CARE AFTER GATHERING

This herb can be used fresh or dried in tea. It has a tart, berry-like flavor and is very high in vitamin C. I enjoy this herb in a mixture with Rose Hips and lemon peel, sweetened with honey.

The dried leaves are more soluble and will keep for about a year if properly stored away from light.

COMMON COMPANION HERBS

Arnica, Oregon Grape, Cleavers, Penstemon, Valerian...

PLANT/ANIMAL INTERDPENDENCE

Our animal and insect companions enjoy the leaves and fruits of this plant as well as we do, and are far more dependent upon it.

This plant stands up well to freezing temperatures. It is one of the first new greens to appear in spring, and among the last to die-back in the fall. I have often seen deer, grouse and other animals digging through the snow, well into December, in search of nutritious Strawberry leaves.

IMPACT CONSIDERATIONS

Wild Strawberry is abundant and in fact quite profuse in some areas. It is fairly resilient to human impact, and it is frequently seen growing in disturbed areas such as along road margins and around old logging slash piles. But before we run out to get our share of Wild Strawberry leaves and fruit, we must first consider the needs of our animal companions and put our impact into a comparative perspective: a single fruit may please our tongue for a few delightful seconds, but the same berry can sustain a small, hungry bird for a week.

Watch the stands of Wild Strawberries in your chosen bioregional niche and identify the needs of our natural friends before you pick.

Wild Strawberry

PHOTO REFERENCES
> *Nature Bound Pocket Field Guide,* Ron Dawson
> *Forest Wildflowers,* Dr. Dee Strickler

TECHNICAL REFERENCES
> *The Herb Book,* John Lust
> *Medicinal Plants of the Mountain West,* Michael Moore
> *Peterson Field Guides – Eastern/Central Medicinal Plants,* Foster & Duke
> *Edible and Medicinal Plants of the Rocky Mountains and Neighbouring Territories,* Terry Willard Ph.D. (also has a good photo)

STAND LOCATIONS

Date of Discovery	Location and Description of Stand	Site Record #

Willow

Salix spp.   Salicaceae

IMPACT LEVEL: 2

DESCRIPTION

The Willow Family (including members of the *Populus* genus) represents over 350 species across North America. Eighteen species of Willow *(Salix spp.)* live in West-Central Montana alone. Furthermore, Willows are known to interbreed and often differ according to specific biological and geographical niches, so I cannot identify all of them here.

Most Willows occur as large shrubs, and are commonly recognized by their catkins (as in "pussywillows") and their common association with water. Leaves are often lanceolate and somewhat similar to those on peach trees, but also vary considerably between many species.

Buy a good Tree Guide (see "Photo References" section of this profile) to identify Willows of your bioregion.

HABITAT

Willows are *very* common just about anywhere there is an available source of water, or where soils retain water over long periods of time (such as north-facing draws where the soil contains alot of clay).

Several species of this huge genus can be found at any elevation in North America; from below sea-level, to near 10,000'.

ACTIONS

Willows contain *salicin,* a salicylic acid-bearing glycoside that acts as an analgesic. In fact, salicylic acid is

Willow

the basis from which aspirin was derived.

Other actions of Willow: anti-inflammatory, antipyretic, astringent, antiseptic.

PROPAGATION & GROWTH CHARACTERISTICS

Willows are very successful and persistent plants. They reproduce from root runners or by seed, and many varieties can be started by simply placing cuttings of the young branches into a glass of water until they take root. They are fast growers too. Many of the erect, shrublike varieties such as *S.exiqua* or *S.scouleriana* can grow to their original height in just two years after being cut cleanly down to the ground. A couple of years ago, I used some of the young, arrow-straight Willow branches for pea stakes. When I pulled them up during the fall, I was amazed to see that they had taken root!

Several varieties of *Salix species* are available through your nursery, and are an excellent choice for a quick-growing privacy barrier around the house. All they really need is water.

GATHERING SEASON AND GENERAL GUIDELINES

The best time to gather Willow bark is during the spring; after the catkins are finished and the leaf buds are just beginning to open. This is when the cambium (inner bark) is transferring the heaviest concentration of water and nutrients from the roots to the leaves, and these elements include the medicinal constituents as well. The bark is much easier to collect during the spring, and can be lifted off by simply cutting small rectangles (1"-4" long) along *one side* of a small (1"-2" wide) limb. *Do not cut completely around the circumference of a limb, or you will kill it...* limit your cut to no more than 1/3 of the circumference.

Another option is to clip ¼"-½" twigs from a few of the limb ends and shave them with your pocketknife. Regardless, the part you want is the greenish inner bark, *not* the tough inner tissue (wood).

Willow

Cut conservatively from several trees and monitor the effects of your cutting throughout the year. There should be no interference in growth.

PARTS USED
The bark, and to lesser effect the leaves.

CARE AFTER GATHERING
The bark can be used fresh or dried in decoctions, but is always better if used fresh. The fresh bark can also be tinctured: 1:2 ratio, 50% alcohol.
Dry the bark in an open paper bag or on butcher paper. Once it is *fully dried*, it can be stored for use throughout the remainder of the year.

PLANT/ANIMAL INTERDEPENDENCE
Willows are important sources of forage for just about any variety of herbivore. In early spring the young shoots are a long awaited source of energy for winter-weary animals that have likely fed on only the bark during the months past. The leaves will then remain as a primary food source until the following winter.
It is interesting to note that when this valuable source of food becomes compromised by heavy foraging, it becomes inedible until new balances are established. This characteristic contributes to cyclic, natural die-offs that keep animal populations in check.
Willows are very strong and resilient, providing a safe haven for nesting birds, rodents, and insects. The erect, shrub varieties common to wet draws and riparian habitats of the Mountain West collect much of their own debris in their lower branches, creating specialized habitat for a wide variety of these creatures.

IMPACT CONSIDERATIONS
Although this herb is profusely abundant, its contributions to members of its biocommunity are critical

268

Willow

ones that deserve our respect. As symbiotic members of the biocommunity, we must always be perceptive of increases in animal and insect dependencies. If the Willows in your area are being devoured or animal populations (such as rabbits) are increasing rapidly, ease the plant's burden by seeking an alternative or by doing without. When gathering from stands where you are aware of nesting or foraging animals, also take into account the *psychological* impact your presence may have upon them. Remember the Anthropocentric Beast...

PHOTO REFERENCES

The Audubon Society Field Guide to North American Trees - Western Region, Elbert L. Little

...or any number of illustrated field guides that focus on trees.

TECHNICAL REFERENCES

Medicinal Plants of the Mountain West, Michael Moore

The Holistic Herbal, David Hoffmann ("Black Willow")

Discovering Wild Plants, Janice J. Schofield

The Healing Herbs, Michael Castleman

The Herb Book, John Lust

Rodale's Illustrated Encyclopedia of Herbs, Rodale

Quick Reference - Medicinal Plants of the Northern Rockies, Mary Wulff-Tilford

Willow

STAND LOCATIONS

Date of Discovery	Location and Description of Stand	Site Record #

Field Notes

Yarrow

Achillea millefolium   Compositae

IMPACT LEVEL: 2

OTHER NAMES
White Yarrow, Milfoil, Soldier's Woundwort, Thousand-leaf, Field Hop, Sneezeweed.

DESCRIPTION
Yarrow is an erect "weed" that can grow to about 3' in height. It has wooly-hairy stems and distinctive leaves that are characteristically "feathery" in structure.

The alternate leaves are narrow and bluntly lance-shaped, and are very finely divided.

The tiny, white to slightly pinkish flowers are borne in flat, terminal clusters. Each cluster may have hundreds of these tiny flowers, and individual plants may bear a dozen or more clusters. Hence, "millefolium" translates to "thousand flowers".

The entire plant is very aromatic, with a distinctive odor that is reminiscent of moth repellent. In fact, Yarrow *does serve as an excellent moth repellent!*

HABITAT
Yarrow is common and widespread across North America in dry meadows, hillsides, vacant lots, and gardens.

ACTIONS
Diaphoretic, hypotensive, astringent, antiseptic, diuretic.

PROPAGATION & GROWTH CHARACTERISTICS
Yarrow is a rhizomatous perennial that reproduces

Yarrow

readily from its tiny seeds. Although it is considered a troublesome weed by many, it is not really as competitive as it is prolific, and generally does not compromise neighboring plants.

If you choose to introduce this plant into the herb garden, keep in mind that each plant will produce *thousands* of seeds that are the size of salt granules (in other words, plan on its long-term residence).

Young plants can be easily transplanted, or the seeds can be planted directly into the garden. To gather the seeds wait until the flowerheads are just beginning to dry, then clip one or two off and put them into a paper bag to dry out completely. Don't pull your hair out trying to separate the seeds from the flower petals, just dump the whole mess where you want Yarrow to grow.

Yarrow has a delightfully long and prolific bloom period. Flowers usually appear mid-spring and last through August. Clipping the top flowers often results in side shoots and *more* flowers.

GATHERING SEASON AND GENERAL GUIDELINES

Gather Yarrow anytime during its bloom period. Using sharp clippers remove a few flowerheads from several plants, leaving plenty for reseeding and pollinator activity.

If you are planning to make a tincture, cut mature plants at least 6" above ground-level. By using the leaves and all, you can eliminate impact upon surrounding vegetation by concentrating your harvest to fewer plants.

PARTS USED

Primarily the flowers for use in tea, but the leaves are useful too and should not be wasted if cut

The entire above-ground plant can be used for tincture.

CARE AFTER GATHERING

Like many herbs, Yarrow is more water soluble and is

Yarrow

better tasting after it is dried. The flowers dry quickly and should be stored in an airtight container shortly after drying is complete. Properly stored, the dried herb will last for about a year, but it tends to turn into dust after longer periods of time... so don't gather more than you need.

For tincturing, all aerial parts may be used. TINCTURE FRESH HERB: 1:2 Ratio; DRIED HERB: 1:5 Ratio, 50% (100 Proof) alcohol.

COMMON COMPANION HERBS

Balsamroot, Penstemon, Mullein, Arnica, Oregon Grape, Horehound, Knapweed...

PLANT/ANIMAL INTERDEPENDENCE

Yarrow is seldom foraged upon, but it serves dual roles in insect/plant interdependency. Although the pungency of this plant repels many types of insects, it is very attractive to others. This selective function of attracting certain insects while keeping others away provides a balance of biodiversity that is beneficial not only to the plant itself, but also to its neighbors. The sudden removal of this plant from its biocommunity may have a sudden and profound impact upon companion plants and other organisms.

IMPACT CONSIDERATIONS

Beware of the possible presence of herbicides when wildcrafting Yarrow, particularly where it is growing in cultivated areas or among other "troublesome weeds."

Before gathering this herb, take extra time to remember and observe its natural roles. Yarrow is a good teacher of EcoHerbalists; it offers a comprehensible introduction into Nature's complex world of "checks and balances."

PHOTO REFERENCES

The Audubon Society Field Guide to North American Wildflowers, Richard Spellenberg

Weeds of the West, Western Society of Weed Science

Yarrow

Northwest Weeds, Ronald J. Taylor
Peterson Field Guides - Eastern/Central Medicinal Plants, Foster & Duke (also contains some technical info.)

TECHNICAL REFERENCES
The Holistic Herbal, David Hoffmann
Medicinal Plants of the Pacific West, Michael Moore
Herbal Healing for Women, Rosemary Gladstar
The New Age Herbalist, Richard Mabey (also good photo)
The Healing Herbs, Michael Castleman
Edible and Medicinal Plants of the Rocky Mountains and Neighbouring Territories, Terry Willard, Ph.D. (also has a photo)
Quick Reference - Medicinal Plants of the Northern Rockies, Mary Wulff-Tilford

STAND LOCATIONS

Date of Discovery	Location and Description of Stand	Site Record #

Yellow Dock

Rumex crispus   Polygonaceae

IMPACT LEVEL: I

OTHER NAMES
Curly Dock, Sour Dock, Sour Grass.

DESCRIPTION
Yellow Dock is a stout weed which can grow to 4' tall.

Yellow Dock begins as a cluster of long (up to 1'), petiolate basal leaves. The plant then heads skyward, with the alternate leaves of mature plants growing mostly off of the stem. The lower leaves of the plant are largest, and **have distinctively curled margins**. Leaves are progressively smaller toward the top of the plant.

The central stalk of the plant is often rusty-red in color and is quite stout, often remaining erect long after the leaves have died back.

Flowers are presented in large, terminal, spire-shaped clusters that later develop into seeds that often turn shades of pink or red in late summer or fall.

HABITAT
Yellow Dock is a European import that is now at home in moist pastures, vacant lots, and other disturbed areas throughout most of North America. It has found its way into many wilderness areas as well, primarily through livestock transport.

ACTIONS
Alterative, cholagogue.

Yellow Dock

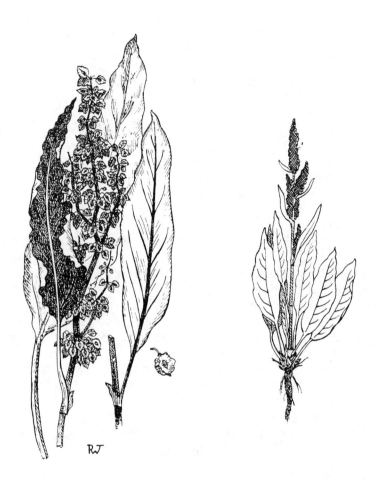

Rumex species

PROPAGATION & GROWTH CHARACTERISTICS

Dock is a perennial in most areas, but may grow as an annual or biennial in areas of extreme climate. It reproduces readily from seed, and is very easy to establish in the herb garden. It will grow in just about any soil, but prefers rich,

Yellow Dock

deep loam. It likes moist conditions, but will endure long periods of drought once it is established.

GATHERING SEASON AND GENERAL GUIDELINES
Gather the roots in the fall, after the plant has gone to seed.

The young, green leaves of this plant are edible. Some people prefer Yellow Dock's robust, tangy flavor over mustard or spinach, but to most the plant is too strong. If you wish to eat some, gather the youngest leaves possible in the spring.

Caution: Dock should be consumed only when the plant is young, and then in moderate amounts. The plant (especially older plants) contains oxalic acid which can be toxic.

PARTS USED
Medicinally: the root. For food: The **young** leaves.

CARE AFTER GATHERING
The roots can be cut into chunks and dried for use in decoctions and infusions. Cut the roots into three or four pieces and spread them out on paper to dry. Properly stored, they should keep for a year or more.

TINCTURE FRESH ROOT: 1:5 Ratio, 50% (100 Proof) alcohol.

COMMON COMPANION HERBS
Dandelion, Mullein, Yarrow, Chickweed, Pineapple weed, Burdock, Goldenrod...

PLANT/ANIMAL INTERDEPENDENCE
Yellow Dock often appears among the first to grow in heavily impacted areas, such as construction sites or plowed fields. Its long taproot penetrates and aerates compacted soils very effectively and helps to prevent erosion in areas where runoff might otherwise present a problem. Like all perennials, Yellow Dock donates its body to the soil every year. It is especially high in iron, a nutrient that is important

Yellow Dock

to plants, as well as people.

IMPACT CONSIDERATIONS
If not targeted itself, Yellow Dock often grows among plants that are constantly assaulted by herbicidal maniacs. Avoid gathering this plant from ditch banks or areas that are actively cultivated. *Always* check on local weed abatement programs before gathering this herb.

PHOTO REFERENCES
Weeds of the West, Western Society of Weed Science
Northwest Weeds, Ronald J. Taylor
Nature Bound Pocket Field Guide, Ron Dawson
The New Age Herbalist, Richard Mabey
Peterson Field Guides - Eastern/Central Medicinal Plants, Foster & Duke

TECHNICAL REFERENCES
Medicinal Plants of the Mountain West, Michael Moore
Discovering Wild Plants, Janice J. Schofield (also has photo)
Menopausal Years, Susun S. Weed
The Male Herbal, James Green
An Elder's Herbal, David Hoffmann
The Herb Book, John Lust
Quick Reference - Medicinal Plants of the Northern Rockies, Mary Wulff-Tilford

Yellow Dock

STAND LOCATIONS

Date of Discovery	Location and Description of Stand	Site Record #

Field Notes

Notes

Appendice I

Bibliography & Recommended Reading

Buchman, Dian Dincin. *Herbal Medicine,* Gramercy Publishing, 1980.

Castleman, Michael. *The Healing Herbs,* Rodale Press, 1991.

Dawson, Ron. *Nature Bound Pocket Field Guide,* OMNIgraphics Ltd., 1985.

Densmore, Frances. *How Indians Use Wild Plants fo Food, Medicine, and Crafts,* Dover Publications, 1974.

Dorn, Robert D.. *Vascular Plants of Montana,* Mountain West Publishing, 1984.

Duke, James A. and Foster, Steven. *Eastern/Central Medicinal Plants,* Peterson Field Guides, Houghton Mifflin, 1990.

Gladstar, Rosemary. *Herbal Healing for Women,* Simon & Schuster, 1993.

Green, James. *The Herbal Medicine-Maker's Handbook,* Simpler's Botanical, 1990.

———. *The Male Herbal,* The Crossing Press, 1991.

Grieve, Mrs. M.. *A Modern Herbal, Vol. I&II,* Dover, 1971.

Hart, Jeff. *Montana - Native Plants and Early Peoples,* The Montana Historical Society, 1976.

Hoffmann, David. *An Elder's Herbal,* Healing Arts Press, 1993.

———. *The Holistic Herbal,* Element Books, 1988.

Hutchens, Alma R.. *Indian Herbalogy of North America,* Shambhala, 1991.

Little, Elbert L.. *The Audubon Society Guide to North American Trees - Western Region,* Knopf, 6th printing, 1988.

Lust, John. *The Herb Book,* Bantam, 20th Ed., 1987.

281

Bibliography

Mabey, Richard. *The New Age Herbalist,* Collier Books, 1988.

Mills, Simon Y.. *Out of the Earth,* Viking, 1991.

Moore, Michael. *Herbal Materia Medica,* Southwest School of Botanical Medicine, 1990.

_____. *Herbal Tinctures in Clinical Practice,* Second Edition, Southwest School of Botanical Medicine.

_____. *Medicinal Plants of the Desert and Canyon West,* Museum of New Mexico Press, 1989.

_____. *Medicinal Plants of the Mountain West,* Museum of New Mexico Press, sixth edition, 1988.

_____. *Medicinal Plants of the Pacific West,* Red Crane Books, 1993.

Reader's Digest. *Magic and Medicine of Plants,* Reader's Digest Books, 1986.

Rodale. *Illustrated Encyclopedia of Herbs,* Rodale Press, 1987.

Rose, Jeanne. *Aromatherapy Book, The,* North Atlantic Books, 1992.

_____. *Herbs and Things,* Grosset & Dunlap - Workman, 1979.

Santillo, Humbart. *Natural Healing With Herbs,* Hohm Press, 9th printing, 1991.

Schofield, Janice J.. *Discovering Wild Plants,* Alaska Northwest Books, 1989.

Schultes, Richard Evans. *Medicines From The Earth,* McGraw-Hill, revised, 1983.

Spellenberg, Richard. *The Audubon Society Field Guide to North American Wildflowers,* Knopf, 1979.

Strickler, Dr. Dee. *Forest Wildflowers,* The Flower Press, 1988.

Taylor, Ronald J.. *Northwest Weeds,* Mountain Press Publishing, 1990.

Tierra, Michael. *The Way of Herbs,* Washington Square Press, 1983.

Weed, Susun S.. *Wise Woman Herbal - Healing Wise,* Ash

Bibliography

Tree Publishing, 1989.

_____. *Wise Woman Herbal - The Childbearing Years,* Ash Tree Publishing, 1986.

_____. *Wise Woman Ways - Menopausal Years,* Ash Tree Publishing, 1992.

Western Society of Weed Science, *Weeds of the West,* revised, 1992.

Willard, Terry. *Edible and Medicinal Plants of the Rocky Mountains and Neighbouring Territories,* Wild Rose College of Natural Healing, 1992.

Wulff-Tilford. *An Herbalist's Quick Reference - Medicinal Plants of the Northern Rockies,* Mountain Weed Publishing, 1993.

Appendice II

The EcoHerbalist's Source List

The following is a list of organizations that promote the preservation of our wild plant allies. It is not a complete list by any means. To identify other sources in your area, check with your local herb retailer, practitioner, health food store, and New Age bookseller.

HERBS, HERBAL PRODUCTS, AND MEDICINE-MAKING SUPPLIES:

Herb Alaska - Canyon Wildcrafts
P.O. Box 15223
Fritz Creek, AK 99603-6223
(Wildcrafted alaska herbs and quality herbal products)

Herbs for Kids
P.O. Box 837
Bozeman, MT. 59717
(Herbs and herbal products focusing upon the needs of children)

Jean's Greens
RR 1, Box 57
Medusa, NY 12120
(Bulk herbs, herb products & containers. No minimum - great service!)

Source List

Montana Botanicals
Box 1365
Hamilton, MT 59840
(Organically grown & wildcrafted Montana herbs)

Rainbow Light
207 McPherson St.
Santa Cruz, CA 95060
(Quality herbs and herbal tinctures)

Sage Mountain Products
Box 420
E. Barre, VT. 05649
(Organically grown & wildcrafted herbs and herbal products, prepared with loving care and many years of experience by Rosemary Gladstar)

Simpler's Botanical
Box 39
Forestville, CA 95436
(High quality herbal tinctures and other herbal products, produced with the Earth and her allies always in mind)

The Herbal Green Pages - Herb Growing & Marketing Network
3343 Nolt Rd.
Lancaster, PA 17601-1507
(An herbal directory that contains thousands of resources)

Wyoming Wildcrafters
Box 874
Wilson, Wyoming 83014
(Quality tinctures and herbal products made from ethically wildcrafted native botanicals)

Source List

SPECIALIZED SUPPLIERS OF SEEDS, NATIVE PLANTS, AND ACCESSORIES FOR THE ECOHERBALIST:

Bitterroot Native Growers
445 Quast Ln.
Corvallis, MT 59828
(This company cultivates and sells an impressive selection of plants that are native to the Rocky Mountain Region)

Garden City Seeds
778 US Hwy 93 N.
Hamilton, MT 59840
(Northern acclimated seeds & supplies, including several hard-to-find heirloom seed varieties. This company is focused on self-sufficient living)

Nichols Garden Nursery
1190 N. Pacific Hwy.
Albany, OR. 97321
(Specializing in herbs & rare seeds)

Peaceful Valley Farm Supply
P.O. Box 2209
Grass Valley, CA 95945
(Tools and supplies for organic farming, plus wildflower seeds and all sorts of handy wildcrafting gadgets)

Prairie Moon Nursery
Route 3, Box 163
Winona, MN 55987
(A cultural guide and catalog of native plants and seeds, geared toward preservation and restoration of wildlands)

Seeds of Change
1364 Rufina Circle #5
Santa Fe, NM 87501
(An environmentally focused supplier of organic seeds)

Source List

INSTITUTIONS OF HERBAL LEARNING:

Australasian College of Herbal Studies
P.O. Box 57
Lake Oswego, OR. 97034
(Offers correspondence courses in natural therapies)

California School of Herbal Medicine
Box 39
Forestville, CA 95436
(Teaches most aspects of herbal study, with strong emphasis upon ethics and Bioregional Herbalism)

Garden Song Herbs
P.O. Box 15213
Fritz Creek, AK 99603
(Owned and operated by herbalist Janice J. Schofield)

Rocky Mountain Center for Botanical Studies
1705 14th St. #287
Boulder, CO. 80304
(Teaches many aspects of herbalism from an Earth-conscious perspective)

Rocky Mountain Herbal Institute
P.O. Box 579
Hot Springs, MT 59845
(Offers correspondence and resident classes in herbal medicine)

School of Herbal Medicine
P.O. Box 168
Suquamish, WA 98392
(Offers correspondence courses in herbal medicine)

Source List

Southwest School of Botanical Medicine
122 Tulane S.E.
Albuquerque, NM 87106
(A highly regarded institute of herbal learning that is owned and directed by herbalist Michael Moore)

The Science & Art of Herbology
P.O. Box 420
E. Barre, VT 05649 *(Herbal teachings by Rosemary Gladstar)*

Wild Rose College
302, 1220 Kensington Rd. NW
Calgary Alberta
Canada T2N 3P5
(Correspondence and resident courses in herbal medicine, directed by Terry Willard, Ph.D.

Mountain Weed Company
HC 33, Box 17
Conner, MT 59827
(Offers classes and field study in herbal medicine, wildcrafting, and EcoHerbalism. Owned and directed by Greg Tilford and Mary Wulff-Tilford)

Appendice III

Glossary

allopathic/allopathy: The use of drugs or other means to antidote a disease or a symptom. The opposite of *homeopathy*.

alluvial/alluvium: sedimentary material (soil, rocks, debris, etc.) deposited by flowing water, as in a delta or riverbed.

alterative: a substance which gradually alters or changes a condition.

analgesic: a substance which relieves pain (aka: anodyne).

anesthetic: decreases sensitivity to pain.

anthropocentric: regarding the human being as the central fact or final aim of the universe.

anti-catarrhal: helps the body rid itself of excess mucus, usually from the respiratory tract.

anti-spasmodic: relieves spasms.

anti-tussive: inhibits coughing.

antifungal: prevents or inhibits fungal infections.

antihidrotic: prevents sweating.

antimicrobial: helps the body resist or destroy pathogenic microorganisms.

antipyretic: lowers fever.

antirheumatic: relieves symptoms of rheumatism.

antiscorbutic: prevents or cures scurvy.

antiseptic: inhibits growth of microorganisms.

antiviral: inhibits viruses.

astringent: tightens tissues; used to check bleeding, diarrhea, etc.

axil: usually refering to the junction where a petiole joins a plant stem.

bacteriostatic: stops multiplication of bacteria.

bitter: triggers digestive process in the mouth.

bitter tonic: an herb that stimulates the secretion of digestive juices; benefits digestion.

carcinogen(ic): cancer producing substance or agent.

cardiac tonic: strengthens or stimulates the heartbeat.

carminative: promotes the expulsion of gas from the digestive tract.

catarrh: the excessive secretion of thick phlegm or mucus by the mucous membranes.

catkin: An elongated, often fuzzy, cone-like flower that generally lacks any distinguishable petals and sepals. Poplars and Willows produce catkins (eg., "pussywillows")

chlorophyll: any of an assortment of green pigments found in plants. Enables plants to convert water & carbon dioxide into carbohydrates.

Glossary

cholagogue: stimulates the flow and secretion of bile.
coagulant: a substance capable of converting blood from a liquid to a solid state.
counter-irritant: an irritant that distracts attention away from another; usually externally applied.
deciduous: the loss of leaves once a year, especially at the end of a growing season.
decoction: an herbal preparation made by boiling the herb in water. This process is often used for bark, roots, seeds, and other hard plant materials that are not soluble enough for use in standard infusions.
demulcent: provides a protective coating and soothes irritation internally.
dermatitis: inflammation of the skin.
detritus: loose fragments that are formed by the disintegration of rocks and forest debris.
diaphoretic: promotes perspiration.
digestive: aids digestion.
diuresis: increased secretion of urine by the kidneys.
diuretic: increases urine flow.
duff: a term used to describe thick mats of leaves and partially composted debris on the forest floor.
Earth regenerator: a plant or other organism that helps to repair damaged habitat and soil structure.
ecosystem: the interdependent interaction between an ecological community and its environment.
emmenagogue: promotes menstruation.
emollient: softens and soothes the skin.
expectorant: helps promote the expulsion of mucus from the lungs; specifically relaxing, stimulating, warming.
hemostatic: checks bleeding.
hypotensive: lowers blood pressure.
immunostimulant: stimulates the immune system
infusion: an herbal preparation made by pouring boiling water over a quantity of herbs and steeping it to extract ingredients (a tea).
lanceolate: lance-shaped; widest at the base, with straight sides long-tapering to a point.
lymphatic: assists lymph system.
micro-ecosystem: a small segment of an ecosystem. When we gather herbs from a specific location (such as a hillside or ravine) we are gathering from a micro-ecosystem.
microcosm: a tiny, often microscopic segment of an ecosystem that represents its own, specialized community of organisms.
mucilaginous: containing or having mucilage - a sticky adhesive substance. Used to soothe inflamed areas of the body.
nephritic: of or relating to the kidneys.
noxious weed: a term used in reference to plant species that are viewed as troublesome to the agricultural and landscape industries.
open-pollinated: plant species that have not been genetically altered (non-hybridized) and are capable of reproducing in true form from generation to generation.
petiole: the stalk, or stem of a leaf, as distinguished from the leaf blade.

Glossary

pH: a numerical measurement of acidity or alkalinity. Most plants grow most efficiently at or near neutral pH levels. A pH level of 7.0 is considered neutral.

photosynthesis: a process by which plants convert solar energy into carbohydrates.

pinnate: a compound leaf pattern where leaflets are *pinnately* arranged along two sides of a stem or axis. **See illustration of ELDERBERRY** for an example.

pollinator-attractor: a plant that is particularly attractive to bees and other organisms that actively participate in the pollination process.

proactive: actions and attitudes that confront events before they occur. The opposite of *reactive*.

raceme: a flower arrangement in which individual flowers have stalks and are attached to an elongated axis or stem. **See FIREWEED.**

refrigerant: cools body temperature by perspiration; same as febrifuge or antipyretic.

rhizome: an underground stem that extends in length horizontally and produces roots, sending shoots upward. Crabgrass presents a classic example.

rubifacient: reddens the skin when applied externally; may cause blistering... use with care.

sedative: calms the nerves.

sepal: a modified leaf, generally green, that encloses the flower bud.

sitzbath: a method of bathing that covers the pelvic region, especially used for genito-urinary and lower abdominal difficulties.

stamen: the male pollen-bearing organ in a flower.

stimulant: a general term for increasing functional activity (refer to specific bodily function)

stratification: a germination process in which a seed must be exposed to a period of cold (often freezing) temperatures and moist conditions to break dormancy.

styptic: an agent that stops bleeding by causing body tissues to contract; generally an astringent.

subalpine: occurring below timberline in the mountains; generally under 9000' in elevation.

symbiosis/symbiotic: the condition in which two dissimilar organisms join together for mutual benefit.

tincture: an herbal preparation made by steeping an herb in alcohol, vinegar, or glycerine.

tonic: a general term for a substance that increases tone; strengthens.

uterine stimulant: stimulates contractions of the uterus.

uterotonic: tonic to the uterus.

vasodilator: dilates/widens blood vessels. Opposite of *vasoconstrictor*.

vulnerary - heals wounds; internal or external.

Appendice IV

General Index

The common name headings of outlined herbs (Part 4) are represented in **BOLD CAPS.** *All plant constituents and botanical names are represented in italics.* Major subheadings are in STANDARD CAPS. *Definitive headings are* Capitalized. **Boldface page numbers denote illustrations.**

Achillea millefolium 271-279
Actions, Medicinal 5
allantoin 137
alteratives 61,195,217,275
ALUMROOT 33-38,35,245
analgesics 95,195
anesthetics 57,169
ANGELICA 39-45, **40, 41,**168
Antennaria species 69-72
anthropocentricity 16-18,21,27
anti-hidrotic 217
anti-inflammatories 47,69,79,89,178,220,238,267
antibacterials 89,164
antigenic protein 230
antimicrobials 52,148,170
anti-rheumatic 100
antipyretics 164,267
antiseptics 57,142,213,217,267,271
antispasmodics 42,66,118,154,178,250
antivirals 148,169
Arctium species 60-64
Arctostaphylos uva-ursi **242-247**
ARNICA 46-50, **47**
Arnica oil 48
Artemesia species 216
Asarum species 199, 253-257
astringents 34,42,69,79,89,123, 173,183,201,205,213,217,220,227, 232,238,243,258,262,267,271
Balsamorrhiza sagittata 51-55
BALSAMROOT 51-55,171
"Bear Medicine" 171

Bearberry **242-247**
Bedstraw, Northern **80,**81
BEE BALM 56-59
berberine 88,89,164
Berberis species 163-167
biodiversity 8
biological herbicides 139
BIOREGIONAL   HERBALISM,   THE
CONCEPT OF 27-28
bitters 61,89,126,142,164
Botanical Names 3
BURDOCK 60-64
calcium 155
*Capsella   bursa-pastoris   224-227,***226**
carcinogenic alkaloids 137
cardiac tonic 154
Care After Gathering (harvesting) 7
carminatives 42,52,57,142,250
cathartic 195
CATNIP 65-68
CAT'S PAW 69-72
*Ceanothus species 172,*212-215
Chamomile 177,178
CHICKWEED 73-77, **74**
Chimaphila species 182-187
cholagogues 89,100, 275
Cicuta douglasii 41, **42**
Clasping Pepperweed 225
CLEAVERS 78-83, **80**
CLEMATIS 84-87
climatic variances 5, 156
coagulants 131
Cocklebur 60

General Index

Comfrey 136, 137
Common Companion Herbs 7
Common Names 3
Conium maculatum 147, 148
coptine 89
COPTIS 88-92
cough 137,138
COW PARSNIP 94-98, **95**, 168
cyclic die-offs 268
Cynoglossum officinale 136-140
cystoliths 233
DANDELION 99-103, **100**
demulcents 75,113,159,195
diaphoretics 42,57,66,85,109,123,169, 271
disinfectants 52,183, 201
diuretics 61,75,79,85,100,109, 123,131,142,154,183,195,205,227, 232,258, 262, 271
Earth regenerators 119,127,158, 161
ECHINACEA 52, 104-106
ELDERBERRY 107-111, **108**
emollients 189, 211
Epilobium species 116-120, 117
Equisetum species 130-135, 132
erosion 36,53,62,102,138,150,191, 277
ethics,defined 22
ETHICAL GUIDELINES, THE LIMITATIONS OF 20-21
ETHICAL GUIDELINES, THE VALUE OF 19
expectorants 42,113,126,159,169, 183, 195
EXPLANATION OF FORMAT *3-12*

FALSE SOLOMON'S SEAL 112-115, 172
Field Pennycress 225
FIREWEED 116-120, **117**
formic acid 230
Fragaria species 262-265
Gallium species 78-83, 80
gastric disorders 34
Gathering Season and General Guidelines 6
giardia 75
Ginger 253, 255
GOLDENROD 121-125, **122**, 246

Goldenseal 91, 92
Goldenthread 88
Goodyera oblongifolia 210-211
guidelines, defined 22
Habitat, Plant 5
Heal-all 220-223
heliosupine 137
hemorrhoidal tissues 174,190, 243
hemostatics 89,131, 217
Heracleum lanatum 94-98, 95
Heuchera species 33-38, 35, 245
HOREHOUND 126-128
HORSETAIL 130-135, **132**
HOUND'S TONGUE 136-140, 172
hypericin 237
Hypericum species 237-241
Hypochaeris radicata 99
hypotensives 250, 271
immunostimulants 52,105, 148
impact 19
Impact Considerations 8
impact formulas 20
impact, intentional 22-24
impact, our perception of 21
impact, unintentional 22, 24-25
impact, vicarious 22,25-26, 28
indigestion 178
interdependencies, organic 202-203
JUNIPER 141-145
kidney disease 142
Kinnickinnick **242-247**
Knapweed 175, 222
Lactuca serriola 99, 100
laxatives 89,100,109,118,154,164, 190, 205
Leonurus cardiaca 153-157
Lepidium perforatum 225
Ligusticum species 168-172
liver stimulant 164
LOMATIUM 146-152, **148**
lymphatic tonics 79, 213
Mahonia species 163-167
Maintaining Records 28-30
Manzanita 183,243,244, 246
Marrubium vulgare 126-128
Matricaria chamomilla 177
Matricaria matricarioides 177-181, 178
medicinal affinities 6
micro-climates 5

293

General Index

microcosms 36, 256
migraine headache 85
Mint family 65,153, 220
Monarda species 56-59
moth repellent 271
MOTHERWORT 153-157
Mountain Ash 107
MULLEIN 158-162
MULTI-LEVEL HUMAN IMPACT 22-26
Mustard family 224
Nepeta cataria 65-68
nephritic 195
nitrates 133
nutritives 100,232, 258
OREGON GRAPE 163-167
OSHA' 168-172
Other Names (plant) 4
oxalic acid 277
PENSTEMON 173-176, 233
Photo References 8
photo-sensitive reactions 96, 239
PINEAPPLE-WEED 177-181, **178**
PIPSISSEWA 182-187
Plant Descriptions 4
Plant/Animal Interdependence 7
Plantago species 188
PLANTAIN 188-192,**189**,210,211, 233
Poison Hemlock 147,148, 169
Pollinator-attractors 44,49,53,58, 57,97,102,110,123,127,156,160, 171,175,218
POPLAR 193-198, **194**
populin 195
*Populus species 193-198,**194**, 266*
Prickly Lettuce 99
Propagation & Growth Characteristics 6
Prunella vulgaris 220-223
Pussy-toes 69
Prayer of the Ancient Ones, 32
PYROLA 185,186,199-204,**200**, 246, 253
Quaking Aspen 193, **194**
RASPBERRY 205-209, **206**
RATTLESNAKE PLANTAIN 210-211
RECOGNIZING THE DISCONNECTED CHILD 13-16
RED ROOT 172, 212-215

RESEEDING, THE REALITIES OF 27
resource management 27
respiratory infections 148, 169
*Rosa species 258-261, **259***
*Rubus species 205-209, **206***
*Rumex crispus 275-279, **276***
SAGE 216-219
Sagebrush 216
salicin 195, 266
Salicylic acid 266
Salix species 266-270
Salvia species 216-219
sambucine 109
Sambucus species 107-111
Saxifrage family 33
secretory stimulant 254
sedatives 66,154,178,205,238, 250
selenium 133
SELF HEAL 220-223
SHEPHERD'S PURSE 224-227, **226**
silica 133
sitz bath 243
Smilacina species 112-115
soil aerators 49,91,114,165, 256
soil compaction 233
*Solidago species 121-125, **122***
Sorbus species 107
sore throat 137
Spotted Cat's Ear 99
Stand Locations 9, **10**
*Stellaria media 73-77, **74***
ST. JOHN'S WORT 222, 237-241
STINGING NETTLE 230-236, **231**
stomach ulcers 79, 190
stratification, cold 70
Streptopus species 112
styptic powder 36, 123
sub-species 5
symbiotic relationships 28
TAMING THE ANTHROPOCENTRIC BEAST 16-18
tannins 34, 243
*Taraxacum officinale 99-103, **100***
Technical References 9
THE REGION COVERED BY THIS BOOK 2
Thistle 175
Thlaspi arvense 225
tonics 123,213,217,220,232, 262

General Index

Twisted Stalk 112
urinary tract infections 201
Urtica dioica 230-236, 231
UVA-URSI 183, **242**-247
uterotonic 89, 207
VALERIAN 248-252, **249**
Valeriana species 248-252
vasodilators, 85, 154, 254
Verbascum thapsus 158-162
vulnerary 47,159,195,220, 238
Water Hemlock 39-41,**42**,94, 96
Wild Candytuft 225
Wildcrafting Log 9, **12**
Wildcrafting Site Record 9, **11**
WILD GINGER 199, 253-257
WILD ROSE 258-261, **259**
WILD STRAWBERRY 262-265
WILLOW 266-270
YARROW 271-279
YELLOW DOCK 275-279, **276**
Xanthium strumarium 60

About the Author and Editor

Gregory L. Tilford has spent every available hour of his life studying the wonders of Nature. Throughout most of his adult years he has shared his experience with others, conducting field studies in wilderness survival, deep-ecology, edible and medicinal plants, and natural attunement. In 1986, he and his wife Mary left the conventions of modern living on a quest to reconnect with Nature. They quit their jobs, packed up their guide books and field notes, and set off for the mountains. In the years that followed they studied and practiced the arts and sciences of self-reliant living as a two person team... Mary as the healer, Greg as the inventor and natural liaison. Together they gained the technical expertise and deep-ecological insight that is contained within these pages.

Greg and Mary continue their lifelong studies at their home in the Northern Rockies of Montana. They teach classes in self-reliant herbalism to learners in their bioregion, and at seminars across North America.

About the Artist

Richard W. Tyler resides in Homer, Alaska, where he maintains an extensive and growing collection of his works in botanical and scenic artistry. His talent, appreciation, and passion for nature's intricacies is a true benefit to Humanity and the Natural World alike.

For self-reliant herbalists...

An Herbalist's Quick Reference to
Medicinal Plants of the Northern Rockies

by Mary Wulff-Tilford

ISBN 0-9638638-6-X

This 20 page book is designed to provide the self-reliant herbalist with a quick reference to medicinal plants of the Northern Rocky Mountain bioregion and much of the western hemisphere.

Hundreds of herb species are represented in over 45 easy to read outlines.

Included are:
- *Common and Botanical Names*
- *Medicinal Actions*
- *Herbal Preparations and Formulas*
- *Dosages and Practical Suggestions*
- *Contraindications*
- *Glossary of Applicable Terminology*
- *Bibliography and Recommended Reference List*

All in a handy size and format for the field-bound herbalist!

Just $3.95 (Ppd)!

Send your check or Money Order to:

MOUNTAIN WEED PUBLISHING
HC 33, Box 17
Conner, MT 59827